EXPECTATION
THERAPY

MASTERING YOUR EXPECTATIONS

EXPECTATION THERAPY

ART COSTELLO

TATE PUBLISHING
AND ENTERPRISES, LLC

Published by Tate Publishing & Enterprises, LLC
127 E. Trade Center Terrace | Mustang, Oklahoma 73064 USA
1.888.361.9473 | www.tatepublishing.com

Tate Publishing is committed to excellence in the publishing industry. The company reflects the philosophy established by the founders, based on Psalm 68:11,
"The Lord gave the word and great was the company of those who published it."

Book design copyright © 2014 by Tate Publishing, LLC. All rights reserved.
Cover design by Joel Uber
Interior design by Jake Muelle

Published in the United States of America

ISBN: 978-1-62994-575-0
1. Psychology / General
2. Psychology / Creative Ability
14.03.11

"Here's to the crazy ones. The misfits. The rebels. The troublemakers. The round pegs in the square holes. The ones who see things differently. They're not fond of rules. And they have no respect for the status quo. You can quote them, disagree with them, glorify or vilify them. About the only thing you can't do is ignore them. Because they change things. They push the human race forward. And while some may see them as the crazy ones, we see genius. Because the people who are crazy enough to think they can change the world, are the ones who do."

—*Steve Jobs*

DEDICATION

To my wife Beverly Mullinax, who has lifted me and held me in her gentle spirit. To my children, Sloane, Corey, and Megan, for inspiring me in a way only children can. To my mother and father, Gertrude A. and Arthur B. Costello, and my brother and sister, Marty and Gert, whose love and support I have cherished. To Charlie Ragus, Oprah Winfrey, and Joel Osteen for lighting the fire of expectation that lies deep in my heart and soul.

To the thousands of people whom I have crossed paths with throughout my life:

You all have had an immense impact on my life's learning.

ACKNOWLEDGMENTS

People who have helped my dream become a reality

- ❏ *Ashley Roy:* You have come to understand me like family because I've opened up to you in so many ways during this journey that we've been on together. It has meant the world to me.

- ❏ *The Tate Publishing family:* This is to each and every one of the staff members because I know what you do is so important to your authors. This journey has been a journey of faith and dedication on everybody's part. Thank you.

- ❏ *My two best friends, Tom Martinez in Santa Ana, California, and Dana Moore in Austin, Texas.* You have listened to me over the years, and for years and years you both have never failed in being supportive. That's what friends do—listen and give advice when asked for *and* needed. You have stuck by my side through so many of life's ups and downs. I love and appreciate you both.

People who have been instrumental in my core growth and development

- ❑ *Pastor Chuck Smith at Calvary Chapel in Costa Mesa, California:* I'll never forget when you baptized me in the Pacific Ocean back in 1969. You have always been an inspiration and a great teacher, not only of the Bible, but of man as well.

- ❑ *Pastor Chuck Swindoll:* When he started in California in a small church with white steeples, there were 100 of us. I watched as the church exploded to 10-12,000 members. Ever since the days you taught my Sunday school, you were and continue to be a true spiritual leader. You have inspired me and grown my faith.

- ❑ *Pastor David Smith at Austin Baptist Association in Austin, Texas:* I can't even begin to explain your role in my life and in my family. You baptized and married my children, buried my wife, and married me to my current wife. You have always been there for my children, my family, and me. You are truly a godly man…the most godly man I know. You have been instrumental in my development and the values that my family have. Your sermons have taught us much, and you are a true friend. I love ya to death.

My Family

- ❑ *My parents, Arthur B. Costello and Gertrude A. Korb Costello*: Thanks for doing the best you knew how to do at the time and for providing for us.

- ❑ *My sister, Gertrude M. Rivoli*: You were a great example of standing tall no matter what life threw at us. Thank you.

- ❑ *My brother, Martin Costello*: Thanks for teaching me what it means to fight for what we want in life and to not cease 'til the Good Lord brings us home to Him.

- ❑ *My wife, Beverly Mullinax*: You have especially been instrumental in my growth. You know how to bring out the best in me and inspire me to keep the faith. I love you.

CONTENTS

CHAPTER 1

A PERSONAL MISSION

"Diminished expectations are like a sword to the heart."

"Expectation" is far more than a word.

It is more than simply imagining an outcome for someone else or yourself.

It is more than an assumption or presumption.

It is more than motivation.

It is not wholly societally imposed.

So what is expectation?

Expectation is our basic root from which we grow. It provides our framework; it is a way of thinking, a way of life. It can limit you and affect the heights of your achievements and your dreams.

Expectation transcends gender, religion, economical and physical abilities, and possibilities. In other words, expectation overshadows everything. It is boundless, profoundly impacting everyone of every culture in every corner of the globe.

Expectation can be our strongest tool or our staunchest foe. If we lower or kill people's expectations, we can control them in a subliminal way. If we continue lowering the expectation for our lives, then soon there is no expectation, and creativity and possibility dry up. We must water our lives with expectation for creativity to flourish. Then we can dream big.

The Expectation Therapy Model was crafted as an impetus to propel society forward. When the necessity of expectation is understood, we can harness it to better ourselves in the workplace, in education, and in every aspect of life. With improved expectations, we create an atmosphere for ourselves to succeed. Expecting the best creates a psychological environment where anything is possible. When we think and believe anything is possible, we can tackle the world with a renewed sense of confidence. Most importantly, the expectations you place on yourself set the stage for your life.

To understand how I've benefited from harnessing the power of expectation, it is first necessary to explain my background, an instrumental part in arriving at the epiphanies supporting this book.

EXPECTATIONS IN MY PERSONAL GROWTH

My parents didn't have stated expectations for my siblings and me. I grew up in a suburban life in New Jersey, and my father was responsible and hardworking five days a week— at least with his job. He was distant from the family. From

5:00 p.m. on Friday until 8:00 a.m. on Monday, he was intoxicated. He was what I'd call a "functional" alcoholic. All of us had our fair share of drama as my siblings dealt with the consequences of their relatively expectation-free existence. However, my grandfather also lived with us and was an entrepreneurial man. I suspect I gained some of my practices from him.

From my birth until age nine, life wasn't too difficult. As the middle child in the family I had a special enthusiasm when it came to baseball. My uncles taught me the basics until I played in the Little League and all but idolized Duke Snider and the Brooklyn Dodgers. I spent every spare minute being active outside, which eventually led to putting into practice my grandfather's influence: I started selling Christmas cards in July. In the '50s, the backs of comic books were plastered with ads. My eyes settled on and mentally circled a certain offer: If I mailed in the coupon, I would receive Christmas cards that I could then sell and send part of the money back to the company. I wasn't even seven years old when I became interested in making a little extra pocket change. It wasn't a great deal of cash, but it was enough.

From that experience I learned to become fearless. My parents didn't go with me; I was this cute little kid probably missing a couple of baby teeth, knocking door to door in hopes of making a sale. Persistently I walked up and down our street, zipping to and fro in optimistic hopes of making a sale.

I'll never forget one particular man. He put his hands on his hips after answering the door and said, "Well, you're a feisty little guy!"

"Yes, sir!" I went on to give him my spiel, and he bought a few boxes from me. Feeling satisfied with the day's winnings, I turned around to leave with pep in my step.

"Wait a sec," the man's voice piped up behind me. "How would you like to have a paper route? I'm the manager of the newspaper's sales division around here, and I like your style."

I explained it sounded fun, but I wasn't old enough—I had to be at least ten years old, after all.

The man smiled, undeterred. "Eh, we can overlook that. You obviously have drive and enjoy what you're doing. Tell you what, I can start you up with ten customers and we will see how you do."

With hard work, he explained, I could build my route to encompass more homes. In that one year, I took my route from ten customers to 165. I was positively ecstatic about it, even hiring my brother (who was eight years my senior) to help me out on Sunday because the newspapers were so heavy and bulky. He didn't complain; I was paying him. Even from a young age, I was somewhat of a visionary.

HOW I HARNESSED ADVERSITY FOR THE BETTER

Art age 8-9

When I was nine, my mother and father sold our house and we moved to the New York countryside, into a dilapidated farmhouse. It was difficult for me to move from everything I knew while I watched the scenery of my hometown shrink in the distance as we drove away. With each mile we drove, I felt pulled in two different directions. My heart tugged at the skyline that faded behind us.

When we arrived, we were considered outsiders. Longtime rural dwellers eyed us suspiciously and greeted us with stone-cold expressions. We didn't know anybody, and nobody seemed to care to introduce him or herself. To make matters worse, there was a void in my life where baseball once was. School bored me—there was nothing challenging about it, as I was not a rote memorization type of person. I processed information differently. I was lonely, bored, and disheartened.

Art & Family Dog
In background is the hill that he climbed
to find peace and comfort

But there was a huge hill next to our house. It was the guardian that kept our farm under its watchful eye. Whenever I looked out my window at the stars, I saw its silhouette, like a resting giant, on the horizon. Somehow

I felt the familiar tugging sensation similar to when we moved from the city. That's when I decided it would become my solace.

Whenever I needed to think, I hiked up that hill, dropped down, and sprawled out on my back. It was my special place. While I stared at the azure sky I felt compelled to speak my heart. It was organic; it felt so natural. I began to listen to an inner voice. Having grown up as a Catholic, I knew I was conversing with God. Just God and me, close and intimate.

"What am I going to become?" I asked as I stared at the cotton-wispy clouds lazily floating by.

"What will my life be like?"

"Will I get married and have children?"

That hill was the silent witness to my self-awareness and saw me develop into the boy on the cusp of manhood— learning to have *faith*. Great things were going to come, but the condition was that I must have faith.

Needless to say, it's challenging to have faith when life isn't going your way. While I was being challenged, I liked to challenge others. That wasn't to my benefit in school because at the time, teachers didn't like to be challenged. Even though ages nine through sixteen weren't my favorite years of life, they did not leave me bitter. It's during the worst times of life that we have the potential to be tempered into the person we're meant to become. As quoted on the website Beyond Ordinary, "God often uses our deepest pain as the launching pad of our greatest calling."

Learning is a positive result of any situation. We gain perspective, and life is all about perspectives. We must use learning for the betterment of our life. When we believe in the value of learning, expectations become high across the board. We expect to learn more because of the value within it. We live a life where everything and anything is possible, but the probability of our dreams' coming to fruition is a choice you or I make! Will we put forth the effort to make it happen? I did, and thus I looked at everything as a lesson ("never a failure, always a lesson" as the phrase goes). With that, even the toughest times fit into my high expectations because of the benefits that inherently accompany learning experiences.

Even though my childhood was tough, my tribulations resulted in a strong work ethic. In turn I instilled the values of a hardworking spirit to my children, and, as I told them, "You can't take shortcuts in a learning life."

Embrace the fact that life is hard and wield it as a learning experience so you can teach other people later on, and move through everything in faith.

As I grew older, I came to realize that God does listen to me. But the reality of life is that He allows us to make choices. He *expects* us to make choices. I loved my parents, but their parenting skills were lacking, to say the least! They would do anything for my brother, sister, and me, but they never verbalized any higher expectations for us.

Living on a farm, we did not have television. I'd meander through the house and trace my fingers along the dusty tables and scan my eyes along the list of titles on our bookshelves. Nothing gave me more pleasure than devouring the classic short story, *The Secret Life of Walter Mitty* by James Thurber (1939). That memorable story was all about his dreams and fantasies. As I curled up in an armchair and thought about the importance of dreams, I knew I had a dream: to become a professional baseball catcher. The vision sustained me and played an important part of my development as a young person.

Art High School Photo

The years passed, but I didn't measure my life in terms of each candle added to my birthday cake. I measured growth in terms of learning experiences, so high school was nothing special for me—a social gathering that I took to high levels of frivolous enjoyment! There was something inside of me telling me that structure and discipline were needed to fulfill my destiny. Still sustained by dreams, I made the decision to join the Marine Corps. That is where I "aged" the most as my eyes opened.

Now, as I said, I've always worked hard. But in the Marines, I quickly discovered the true meaning of hard work, structure, and discipline. Even though we performed seemingly insurmountable tasks in the blood, sweat, and dirt of boot camp, one of the greatest lessons of my lifetime became blaringly apparent:

The words "I can't" exist only in my mind.

I performed physical tasks that I never would have thought I could do. The trick? Putting my mind to it! That's when I realized the limitless bounds of what I could accomplish and gained invaluable lessons with which to better conduct my life. The human mind is a more powerful organ than we can grasp. It controls the body and even our destinies.

LESSONS FROM VIETNAM

Soon the Vietnam War broke out. My lessons were put to the test, but of course my learning wasn't over because it never is. My fellow Marines and I would be walking on a rice paddy, and in a split second, a Marine behind me would lose his life. There are no guarantees for how long we are given on earth. It was a huge, tough concept to accept, but through it I experienced the brotherhood of being a Marine. We learned to value other individuals more than we valued our own lives. As a teenager and child, it was all about me, me, and me. Nothing could teach me more quickly than my experiences in Vietnam that it *isn't* about me. It's about others and what we do for others to help them improve. It's about becoming more than you yourself are.

Art & Youn 1966

In Vietnam, my worldview shifted when I saw Youn. A little orphan girl of about nine years old, she captured me with her moon-shaped, sparkling black eyes. They were beautiful. In the moment I beheld her, I was driven to do whatever it took to make her lot in her war-torn country easier. As soon as I could, I wrote my mother at home to help the effort.

"Mom, we had a dinner with orphans here and I met the most beautiful little girl, Youn. She and these kids need clothes, toys... anything." I thought about the deplorable conditions during this war. What could I do to change another life, even surrounded by such death? Without hesitation I told Mom to take the money from my savings and donate it to the cause, if need be. As it turned out, this was a fruitful endeavor:

Youn Thanksgiving Day meal in line at mess hall

Marine in Vietnam Helps Orphan Girl

For Lance/Cpl. Arthur P. Costello, and probably hundreds of other servicemen who will spend Christmas at war in South Vietnam, the children of Vietnam will be a kind of stand-in for home.

Costello recently wrote his parents, Mr. and Mrs. Arthur Costello, about a dinner given by American Marines for the children of an orphanage near their base 25 miles north of DaNang.

"The Marines were chosen to escort the children around the base and to chow. I got the cutest little girl. I wish you could have seen her.

"She is 9 years old and her name is Youn ... I bought her a toothbrush and soap and a wash cloth and a couple of towels. We ate at the mess hall—turkey and ham and all the goodies that go with it. She had a ball."

"It's hard to explain the feeling I had when I was with her. Not a feeling of boy friend-girl friend," he said, but rather more like father and daughter. *"That's the way I felt and so did a hundred other guys."*

"I'm going to see her as often as possible—can you send some clothes for her? I don't know her sizes, but I'd say she's as big as a five- or six-year-old in the States."

This was a different letter than any his parents had received from their 19-year-old son. "Vietnam has made such a difference in him," his mother said. "That such things would move him. I know he's concerned."

Her son's letter continued:

"If you can't get any clothes for her, take some money out of my bank account and buy her some... please. It would really mean so much to me and to her."

Youn 1966

(Invading Arthur's savings would hardly be necessary, Mrs. Costello assured. She's already begun gathering lightweight clothes, not only for Youn, but other children in the orphanage.)

"It really makes you feel good inside to know that you're helping someone," *Arthur continued... "We still have to go out every other night on patrol."* (He's lost a good friend in an enemy ambush.)

"The nights we don't go on patrol, we worked in our compound. It's getting late now and I've got to try to get some sleep and write more later.

"I hope you aren't worrying."

29

MORE ON YOUN

An appeal by a former Avoca marine has resulted in a deluge of clothing and other essentials, which are being distributed to needy children in Vietnam. Corporal Arthur P. Costello, son of Mr. and Mrs. Arthur B. Costello of 86 Union St., Rochester, formerly of Avoca, asked his mother to send clothes to fit an orphan girl of about six years old.

The girl, Youn, was treated by the corporal to Christmas dinner in the mess hall at his base near Da Nang. He bought her a washcloth, toothpaste, and some soap, and as Corp. Costello said, "She had a ball."

His mother already had sent one bundle of other articles for distribution to Vietnamese children. bundles are being prepared.

Arthur B. Costello thinks response to the appeal to his wife is excellent.

"We had donations from the city of Rochester Greece and Hilton," he said.

Costello has a sister, Gertrude, 17. Perhaps "sister" reminds him of her."

ARTHUR P. COSTELLO

Thanks Donors for Viet Nam Aid:

AVOCA—The family of a former Avocan, now serving in the Marine Corps in Vietnam, has thanked local donors for their aid to Vietnamese children.

The Marine, Corporal Arthur P. Costello, wrote home a few weeks ago asking contribution to aid a 10-year-old girl, Youn, and the other children at an orphanage near his DaNang base.

The appeal was relayed to the Avoca American Legion auxiliary by his parents, Mr. and Mrs. Arthur B. Costello, of Rochester. The auxiliary has collected several pieces of clothing and personal items to be sent to the orphanage, and more are sought.

Eventually, I ended up supporting Youn and funded her as well as her orphanage. Through the length of the war I saw her whenever I could. Unfortunately, the orphanage was destroyed in the war. The children were lost.

Quang Nam Province 1966

We are lucky to live the lives we live in this country. If we go out and see other lands, it quickly becomes obvious that their citizens have fewer opportunities than we do. Their lives are often a matter of survival. The human spirit can survive and transcend any situation; as I learned in the Marines, we can push our bodies past what we ever conceived was possible. It goes back to mind over matter. I had conviction that what I was doing was right. I learned compassion for other people.

Vietnam was life changing. I learned compassion, loving others more than myself, and soaking up the moment. Learning the lesson that life is a series of moments was a huge influence in my life and development as a man. After I came home from Vietnam I worked another year and a half in the Marine Corps, then I got out and decided to go to college and further my education. During college I managed rock-and-roll bands and worked at a mental health center. Each step of life was a formative, life-changing event for me, rich with learning experiences.

Still, the majority of positive learning came out of my Vietnam experience and experience in the Marine Corps. In having lived moment to moment, I discovered that the important aspects of life become evident. The most important part of living is this very moment. "Seize the day," as they say. Expect the unexpected. Obstacles are only as big as we make them. With pride in wearing the uniform, I puffed my chest out and thought, *whatever I do with passion and conviction, I can achieve. I will believe and expect myself to do great things.*

THE "WHAT-IFS"

The realizations from my years as a Marine opened up a floodgate of growth in my young-adult years.

For me, the best method of learning is through experience. I like to read and write, but getting down and dirty with experiences is what motivates me. My experience in the Marines truly got me thinking, and everything came to a head.

What if my parents had set expectations that would have harnessed my abilities to guide my growth and development better?

How would that have changed my path?

Would I have become the professional baseball player I desired to be?

Or could I have been the President of the United States and changed the path of a nation?

What would I have become?

The answer is that I will never know! The other possibilities never came to fruition, and there's no use dwelling on a past that can't be changed. I call this assault on the senses "The What-Ifs." I can remember my first "what if" moment. When I was around five or six, my mother and I were driving down a road. There was a truck in front of us. I can remember it like it was yesterday. It was carrying long sections of pipe around two inches in diameter, and all of a sudden a section of the pipe came loose and flew through the windshield of our car. Let me put this in perspective: It didn't just come through the windshield; it came through the windshield, front seat, back seat, and trunk, impaling the length of the car!

Art at 3 years old

Here's my "what if" moment: my mother and I had been talking as we often did on our car rides in those early years. I would snuggle up to her and put my head on her side and listen to her breathe and her heartbeat. For whatever reason, right before the pipe came loose, I slid over to the passenger window to look at something outside. What if I hadn't moved over those few inches? My life would have ceased—I'd be dead, gone, and buried for the rest of time. That's when I learned about the strength of "What if?"

We all have had these moments: *what if I had done this,* or *what if I had done that?* Would life be different than it is now? You bet it would. I can't count the number of situations that I have encountered that altered results because I chose for some reason to do something at the right place at the right time. A prime example was in Vietnam. One of my fellow Marines would walk ten yards back over the same terrain I had just traveled, would step on a land mine and be maimed or killed. It was hard to understand, but "what if" it had been me?

It's a tough concept to understand, but over time I began to realize that there was something more powerful going on. Some choose to call it fate while others choose to say "s— happens" but I, a different kind of thinker, chose to call them my "what if" moments. I believe that all things happen for a reason, a purpose, and "what if" moments are no different. The big question that arises out of this pattern of thought is, "What is the *purpose*?" I've come to the conclusion that *we aren't supposed to know.* As we live each moment to the fullest, like we are expected to do, life unfolds like a well-developed plan.

∽

These are my core beliefs that I gained from my retrospect on my experiences in Vietnam. After the Marines shaped me into the man I am today, I realized we as parents, teachers, and leaders must start expecting more from those we influence. If we do not expect, we will not achieve. There are no ifs, ands, or buts about it.

Think about your own life. Who in your life set the expectations?

The Marines, the expectation-setters, started me on a path of believing I could be and *would* be great if I simply expected greatness from myself. My challenge in writing this book is, I pray, that I can open your eyes to the value of expectations and the essential roles they play in the development of our spirit and soul, heart and passion.

IN RETROSPECT: THE IMPORTANCE OF EACH MOMENT

My expectations were high, but the Marine Corps set the bar even higher, and my standards shot up across the board. One thing I've learned about myself over the years is that I've developed a mindset for success: living in the moment and not looking back. If we look back and regret something, then we probably shouldn't have been doing it in the first place. The decision to do what we were doing was clearly not the best for that time and place. It all goes back to living in the moment.

Unbelievable as it may seem, I can say with confidence that I've never regretted anything I've done. It's about the perspective we take. One of the keys to living without regret—even if we make a "poor" decision—is to learn to live with it and constantly own it, take responsibility for it, and move forward in confidence. In other words, when we live moment to moment, we learn to adjust to life's events very quickly. With life's events, we take the everyday and even the mundane seriously. I'm constantly making decisions and processing them, so when I act upon them, I am focused on the process and evaluating everything and prioritizing tasks. If we become skilled at prioritizing and understanding what is truly important, we can make important decisions based on a whole number of factors. We have to think rapidly when we optimize each second of the day.

What I've found is that my mindset has been positive because it is based on *faith*. This is not just faith in God, but also those around me and in myself. This is particularly important because we have to trust in ourselves that the decisions we make are the right ones based on the information we have in our heads at that time. Through this faith, I've had a positive mindset that yields positive results. I've treasured the philosophy "I refuse to lose"— not regarding winning or losing, but the importance of refusing to let the negatives rule my thought processes. If I do miss something then I believe I have lost an opportunity to learn. That goes back to moment-to-moment living. It even irritates me when I don't learn from an experience! I equate losing to not learning something and missing out on an experience because learning has been experiencing the moments that add up to make hours, days, weeks, months, years—in other words, life! Everything is about learning.

How did I learn this? Much of my rapid decision-making technique blossomed in the military because when I was in the service, my actions affected other people's lives. I learned it out of necessity! The ever-present possibility was not only that I could lose my own life but cause loss of life to my fellow men.

When my son was ten or twelve years old, we went to the Vietnam Veterans Memorial in Washington D.C. I led him to the front end of the wall. He looked down the glinting monument at the 58,000 names engraved on it and made a comment I'll never forget: "Dad, I didn't realize that 58,000 names could look so big. When you stop and think about it, each one of these men had a sister, brother, grandparents, and parents. Each death affected so many people."

He was so right. We were both young at the time, but it astounded me that he could comprehend the idea that so many lives are affected by war and the loss of life. When we put the numbers of the people affected into perspective, it's surreal.

The author Andy Andrews wrote *The Butterfly Effect*, one of my favorites. Within its pages he explores how human lives are affected by every event and experiences that happens, creating a ripple effect throughout eons and eons of time. That was one of the things that I took away from my military experience: everything we do has an effect not only on ourselves, but also on those around us for lifetimes. It has been a major consideration throughout my life.

Similarly, when I meet somebody, I often wonder if they realize the effect of what they're saying and how it affects others around them. People have the tendency to be oblivious about simple things such as the speech they produce and the tone, style, manner, and attitude with which they speak. If we all become more conscious about what we say, we eventually are creating a better overall awareness. That's just another example of how to adjust moment-by-moment staying aware of our audience and acting and speaking accordingly.

Every event in my life has brought me to this particular point in my existence on earth. Every learning experience I've had has brought me to this very moment in time. Everything we do and everything we are culminates to where we are and whom we are, creating an effect across the spectrum of life. When we become aware of it and the magnitude of what each action and word means, then digesting it and working through it becomes meaningful to the mind, the spirit, and the way we live.

CONCLUSION

My experiences growing up and particularly in the Marines altered my worldview, and I began to harbor the ideas I am presenting to you in this book. In review:

❑ Expectations provide a framework for life! The importance of expectations is paramount for anybody who walks this earth.

❑ My becoming fearless early on through selling cards and my paper route allowed me to set my expectations high.

❑ The Marines proved that there is no truth to the phrase "I can't." Accepting this helped me to believe in setting expectations high.

❑ If you believe in the value of learning, then you aren't dismayed by expectations that haven't been met. You come out of a situation much wiser and refueled for reaching your dreams. This is also why you must adjust expectations on a moment-by-moment basis, paying attention to your surroundings and situations.

❑ Living in the moment helps you prioritize and pursue life and your expectations without fear.

❑ Do not slow down because of the "what ifs." Instead, let the outcome of each event reinforce the fact you are meant to be here and reach your dreams.

❑ Think about the butterfly effect. Each decision you make has consequences and touches others for generations. Everything you do spans a great length and width of time; let that empower you to expect the most!

❑ Most importantly, trust yourself! If you don't, how can you expect to reach your goals? Trust yourself and use your best judgment. Simply being self-aware works wonders.

This chapter details how I've arrived at the tenets in my life that I hold dear. They have helped me become a successful man with a zeal for life, love, and learning. When there are expectations to be met, the course of your life changes for the better and enriches you as a human being. To better understand how to live the life you want and become fulfilled, let's jump into the nitty-gritty of expectations.

Chapter 2

What are Expectations?

What comes to mind when you think of expectations? Most people perceive expectations as imposed by others, perhaps a child presenting a test packet with a big, fat, red "F" on it to his or her parents. Then the parents' faces turn violet as they exclaim, "We *expect* more of you than that!" Perhaps another set of parents is leaving to go on a date. Before they leave, they remind their children that they *expect* them to behave.

Expectations are implicit, too. When a man and woman marry, the expectation in their vows is that they will be faithful to one another, even when the times are tough—in sickness and in health. The expectation assigned to a handicapped parking space is that only handicapped people with a handicap tag will use them. Drivers expect the oncoming traffic to stay on the other side of the road.

When we think about it, these implicit expectations govern the details of our everyday lives. Expectations are why there is order and why chaos doesn't run rampant. Expectations abound in relationships—both familial and romantic—and in just about every sphere of society: the workplace, education, the law, sports, and religion.

Think for a moment on the origin of expectations. By the Christian worldview, God made Adam and Eve and expected them to tend to the planet and the animals upon it. Additionally, they were not to eat the fruit of the tree of the knowledge of Good and Evil that grew in the middle of the Garden of Eden. This is the first model of expectations that we have. It is from God that we gain a sense of purpose through His expectations for us. It is also important to note that God is *above* expectations; according to the Amplified Version of the Bible, He "is able to carry out His purpose and do superabundantly, far over and above all that we dare ask or think" (Ephesians 3:20).

Clearly it's more than just a word, but the root of *expectation* is defined by Merriam-Webster as, "a strong belief that something will happen or be the case in the future," and "a belief that someone will or should achieve something." Expectation is the impetus for performing an action—for the purpose of achievement. Without expectation, we're purposeless, afloat in the sea of life.

Think back to the anecdotes at the start of the chapter. The achievement the parents hope their children will gain is an A on a test. In turn the A leads to a better final grade in the class. In the long term, grades lead to better opportunities, such as acceptance into accredited colleges and increased chances for stable jobs. Again, we can see how one action has a butterfly effect. Digesting the definition and visualizing relevant scenarios are how we can make sense of the meaning of expectation in its basic form, but it is more than meets the eye. In actuality, it is a massive concept that has widespread implications for our lives and the way we conduct them. When we understand not only the meaning of expectations, but how it also feeds into our outlooks and outcomes, we have acquired one of the most valuable tools for our lives.

EXPECTATIONS AS A PRINCIPLE AND THEORY

Action is the central ingredient for expectations. Expectations without an action are merely a thought—something we do all the time! We have millions of thoughts every day, but unless we match action to a few of the "good" ones, they don't really become an expectation that makes our goals happen.

One conclusion I've made is that in order to achieve our expectations, we need to have a plan of action. First of all, it needs to be well thought out. Personally, I think it helps to write my expectations down in the form of goals, desires, needs, and wants, because if I don't, then it doesn't become a part of my life as a driving motivation. I've written down my goals and what I wanted to achieve, and that helps me meet my expectations. It keeps my "eyes on the prize."

Have you ever made lists on sticky notes of the day's goals and stuck them to your computer monitor? That's the same idea! It's your goal that you expect to meet.

Viewing the execution of expectations through this lens helps transform them into an attitude, almost a way of living, especially if we develop our expectations on a daily basis and through moment-by-moment responses. There are new expectations to form, and we can build upon preexisting expectations to keep them relevant and keep us focused on our desired results.

FAITHFUL VS. FEARFUL EXPECTATION

Expectations are based on two central perspectives in the mind that affect how we approach them. The first lens through which to approach expectations is *faith*. Faith can come in many forms. For me it has been faith in God. For someone else it might be faith in a parent, faith in a teacher, or something similar. Honestly, though, I think that if all of us were to stop and examine our expectations and look at where the root of them comes from, we would find they are deeply seated in a faith that we have in ourselves, in God, and/or in others around us.

If all the while we keep the highest expectations derived through faith in those around us and ourselves, those optimistic thoughts create a self-fulfilling prophecy. Everything moves forward and upward in a positive way.

The reverse of that is if we enter expectations fearfully, basing them on fear instead of faith. Fear causes hesitation and consternation; it blocks potential for positive thinking and causes the human mind to falter and question its capabilities. When we start questioning and hesitating, it compounds into a million excuses to not take action that is positive. Self-doubt creeps into our minds until it paralyzes us.

Overall, fear is destructive to the human mind and therefore to positive thinking itself. Why? I believe that positive expectations create creativity itself—it loosens the inhibitions of the mind so it creates an optimal environment to start thinking creatively and innovatively. Then the processes in our lives change. When we act fearfully, it causes paralysis so we can't move forward and progress. It not only leads to self-doubt and depression, but also the people around us lose faith in our abilities! Others can tell when we don't believe in ourselves.

On the other hand, when we move with high expectations in a positive manner, it becomes contagious! That's why it's so important in our country and community that we have people who constantly drive our expectations higher because that's where our creativity lies, problem solving is accomplished, and how the human mind starts solving problems creatively. We become sharper, better people for it; there's an infinite amount of good that grows from positive expectations.

Say you get to college and want to join an organization. You like the idea of college marching band, but you don't know an instrument. If you believe you can learn one, you easily build a plan of action—renting a saxophone, enlisting the help of a music veteran, booking lessons with that person. Thus your goal of making the band is more likely to happen. But without faith, how would the scenario play out? If you didn't believe it would happen, you probably wouldn't delineate a plan of action. Fear stifles creativity, after all, so you wouldn't have the positive fuel to construct and drive down a path. If you still went through the motions but didn't believe in yourself, then the fear would almost certainly kill your morale. You'd be less likely to practice the instrument. In your fear you'd be less focused on the goal than the fear itself.

Fear paralyzes us with its diminished expectations. And don't forget that "diminished expectations are like a sword to the heart" because they kill the human spirit and creative thinking processes and stop us dead in our tracks.

Think about it. When we pay attention, we can rapidly pick out someone who has low expectations when we hear them speak. Listen for hesitation. On the flip side, listen to somebody with positive expectations. There's a particular radiance around them, a glow that comes from having high expectations. They are confident in themselves and put us at ease. Because positive or negative expectations communicate a nonverbal message to others, how we channel our positive expectations becomes essential in everyday life and increases the likelihood of their coming to fruition.

MAINTAIN AN OPEN MIND IN YOUR FAITH

So far it's easy for you to gauge that I'm not a fearful person, meaning you have probably assessed that I don't react to events in my life from a point of fear. Faith has dominantly defined how I respond to life. That being said, one of my other places of reference is open-mindedness. I've been concerned about failing to remain open-minded and consequently missing out on an outstanding learning experience or life-altering opportunity.

When I meet people I enter into the exchange with an open and clear mind and evaluate body language, eye contact, and verbiage. I want to understand their background and anything along the way that will give me a better and clearer understanding of how that person thinks. We all have lived varied and different lives, so each person has a unique set of details in their life that makes them react or respond differently to events and opportunities presented to them on a daily basis.

Being open-minded gives you the opportunity to learn at every turn in life. You are able to see what others choose to shut out since they don't give the other person's point of view a chance. The mere existence of my personal blog is a testament to my open-mindedness. Listening to Oprah Winfrey and Joel Osteen doing an interview was the inspiration for my blog and this book. Had I closed my eyes and ears to the possibilities that lay ahead, I would not be on this extraordinary journey I am now traveling. When I look back on my life and mentally assess all I have done, I am in awe of what I would have missed had it not been for my receptiveness to the possibilities of the unknown opportunities in the future.

One of the most joyful experiences in my life thus far was meeting my current wife after the loss of my previous wife of thirty-five years to ovarian cancer. If I had not been open-minded toward online dating sites and responded to an ad she placed on Match.com, we would not be together now, happily married and as fulfilled as two people could ever be. She is a prayer answered, my expectation met, and my gift from God. She has added tremendous value to my life, and to my children's and grandchildren's, but most of all to me. She is an encourager of a magnitude unknown to me ever before in my life.

I shudder to think of what my life would be like and what I would be missing out on if I didn't have open-mindedness. My life certainly would not have taken the course it has without her love and support.

Most importantly I've learned that open-mindedness leads us in directions that can have extreme benefits and life-altering opportunities if we let it. Having faith is the comfort of knowing that in the big scheme of life, all will be right in the end. I am blessed every moment of my life in so many ways by recognizing that this, right here and right now, is where the joy is and blessings lay.

On the other side of the coin is closed-mindedness. This has a safe feel to it for many people who don't take a chance and don't experience new things for fear that they might be harmed in some way. Therefore, it all becomes a matter of mindset regarding expectation. My premise with expectations has been that either you can move forward in faith or be halted by fear. This is the ultimate choice we make. My hope and prayer for each and every one of you is that you will learn to expect with faith and fear nothing, catapult your dreams and joys to new heights, expect to be blessed in all you do, and react with open-mindedness to learn new things in life. This is what I call living life to the fullest.

THE IMPORTANCE OF CREATIVITY

If positive expectations drive creativity and help it thrive, then we must also ponder why creativity is important. It's quite simple: life *is* creation. We are created, and everything around us is created impeccably. In turn we are creatures endowed with the ability to mimic our maker and create works of aesthetics, value, and/or utility. Important for our daily endeavors is that "Being creative keeps you motivated in what you love doing, it keeps you fresh and on your toes" (Morton, 2013).

Creativity feeds motivation, which is an ingredient of success. Positive expectations inherently sit hand in hand with visions of our preferred outcomes. We must then think through ways to reach that outcome (creativity)—and when we're positive, we more easily analyze the situation and ways to reach the desired outcome (think back to positive expectations freeing the mind and letting creativity run wild). The possibility of that outcome therefore nourishes our motivation.

Think of it this way: say you want to earn a raise at work. You know you have the talent and the work ethic. You *believe* you can do it, so you expect that outcome for yourself. Plus, the idea of a little extra cash is motivating! Then you start brainstorming—"How can I best reach that goal?" That's when the creative juices start flowing. You outline a schedule that allows you to maximize your time and begin your day by establishing the right tone. The first five minutes can break or make your day—will you jump into work or drag into it? You reason to yourself: *If I start my day on "the right foot," it'll be easier to run with that.* From the minute you step in the office, you expect more of yourself. From there you add more detail to that plan. Instead of spending twenty or so minutes gabbing in the break room in the morning while you grab coffee, you start spending only five minutes in the break room. You brainstorm how to better communicate and work with your time. It goes from there.

If positive expectations nurture creativity, then creativity helps expectations become a reality. They each work together in a symbiotic relationship. In that case, how can we become creative? By constructing positive expectations we are able to truly tap into our creativity and get the most out of it:

❑ *Keep a notepad.* This way we can scrawl down creative ideas as they come to us. Have you ever had a light bulb moment and forgot what it was whenever you finally put pen to paper? This eliminates that problem. Some stores sell waterproof notepads so you can even write your ideas in the shower.

❑ *Try drawing instead of verbalizing.* When an idea pops up, initially it is not associated with the left side of the brain involved in verbalizing ideas.

❑ *Move away from your interests.* It sounds counter-intuitive, but sometimes it helps breed more creativity if we move away from our area of interest. While writing this book on expectations, I looked beyond the area of discipline people might expect of expectations—subjects like psychology—and even moved into physics! This only further solidified my hypotheses.

❑ *Ask questions.* As Morton says, "When you don't accept the status quo, your brain has to come up with an alternative" (2013). We keep ourselves sharp when we look beyond the current situation to a world of possibilities. There's certainly more than one way to look at something, but we must find it through curiosity.

❑ *Get bored.* When we don't focus on the task at hand and let our minds roam, sometimes we stumble upon the answers and the ideas we sought while previously under pressure. (Shower epiphanies are a great example!)

Positive expectations drive me to find creative solutions so that many of the above ideas become integrated into my practice. Think back to my "What if"-ing thoughts: *What if I choose this, or what if I do that differently?* This has sculpted my thought process and brought me to think in a different way, exploring the different side of the unknown. I have embraced my way of thinking but it sure has stirred up some conventional thinkers' brains!

In sum, there are endless ways to nurture a sense of creativity; different methods work for different people. Positivity waters the gardens of our minds while negativity uproots them. When we're positive and believe anything can happen, we find many ways to make dreams become reality.

∽

When we nurture positive expectations, start writing them down, and move forward, we begin to fulfill the prophecy that we have for ourselves. I firmly believe we *are* what we think we are. Likewise, we *become* who we think we are. When we are positive, we will experience positive outcomes and have positive influences around us. It compounds, like the butterfly effect I mentioned earlier. Our outlook, and therefore our situation in life, affects our family and everyone around us—it even affects our health! Why do you think stress takes a toll on our physical wellbeing? It lowers the immune system and even makes us sick—all because we view our life's load as more than we are able to handle in our given environments.

If we believe we can do something, then that certainty eliminates the stress (the bad kind, at least; some healthy stress can be helpful). The more unfavorable situations and feelings that overcome and overwhelm us, the more we need to look for the positive end. Adversity will come to pass. Be positive, be strong, and it will shine through us and endow us with power. Expectations can create a power like we've never known before. We just have to believe that we can and will have a positive outcome. Remember: learning from adversity builds stronger expectations and character, which creates strength of mind.

MORE ON FAITH:
WHY IT IS *ESSENTIAL*

Faith is of utmost importance when seeking to understand expectations and how they affect us. In order to harness expectations to create desired results in life, as we will discuss in detail later, we must first look at the Law of Expectations:

> The Law of Expectations says that, basically, we get what we expect out of life. We tend to see what we expect to see, we tend to feel what we expect to feel, we tend to act the way we expect to act, and eventually, we tend to achieve what we expect to achieve. Your expectations influence your happiness and, they influence your health. Your expectations influence your relationships. (Santos, 2013)

The reach of expectations is wide and far. To approach it with fear would affect countless avenues in life and, as we discussed earlier, imprint our future with doubt, hesitation, and inaction, and thus a high probability of failure.

Here's what we need to understand about fear, the opposite of faith: Fear is the most destructive and commonly used tool to destroy man's creativity. It is the complete opposite of faith. Governments, religions, parents, teachers, and anyone who wants to control people use fear! Salespeople use the fear of loss to invoke buyers to make a purchase; teachers use grades as a system to control their students and parents. Why do you think they use it? To prevent unwanted results! Government uses fear of loss to control the masses and instill in the population that they are unable to take care of themselves or their community. This gives the government its role and power. Religion, for the most part, has used fear to control the masses through the loss of God's favor—i.e., if you don't attend church or tithe or read the word of God, then God will withhold His grace and favor toward you. These are tools used to control man through the tactic of fear, which is prevalent across all cultures and communities.

We have a choice to submit to and believe in the fears that are instilled in our world, or we can choose to live by faith.

Faith derived from the belief in oneself or others will create an environment of wellbeing and security in our inner self. Faith is the cornerstone of expectations that are positive and creative. All expectations are based on these two lenses through which to look at the world and ourselves: fear and faith. If you act on your expectations from a base point of fear, then the negative is the byproduct. If you act on expectations from the base point of faith, positive results follow.

It's also important to note that, as Joel Santos says, "When you expect the best, you're honoring God" (2013). I believe expecting the best shows trust in Him! As in any relationship, we desire mutual trust. It reveals trust in the perfection of His plan and that He wants the best for us, so we pursue that with trust in our God-given abilities. Santos also reminds us to think of David and Goliath as an example: David either could have been intimidated by Goliath's size, or he could have approached it by realizing Goliath's size made him an easy target for his slingshot. It's all about perception.

David Foster Wallace made a commencement speech at Kenyon College called, "This Is Water." In it he describes the mundane and seemingly endless routine of the average workday—sitting in unmoving traffic, dodging fellow customers in the too-crowded supermarket, and other banalities. Once we actively shift our perspective, though, it's easier to get by. We notice that everyone else is in the same boat: Getting to work to make a living. Buying groceries at the one time of day that they can—which happens to line up with everyone else's. Actively working to switch our perspective can happen by choice. This is just one example of that. Over time, working toward a faithful perspective can and does become easier.

Now, it's natural that fear will rear its ugly head every so often. The important part is to jump back on the train of faithful thinking. Finding faith is an ongoing cycle to incorporate into daily practice. When we give in to fear, the situation starts looking like Pandora's box as tons of scary possibilities freeze us in terror. Remember:

"Whether you think you can, or you think you can't—you are right."

—Henry Ford

In wrapping up this section on faith, commit to memory that you are in total control of your future because of your faithful or fearful expectations. Your mind confines you or sets you free. "If you have low expectations for yourself, you will NOT work to reach higher levels of abilities" (Mr. Andrews, 2013). You literally unconsciously prevent yourself from succeeding if you are too afraid to create higher expectations for yourself and dream big! If you don't believe in yourself, who will? How will you accomplish great things?

CONCLUSION

Expectations are from the beginning of time and span across the ages, are both stated and implicit, and have a wide impact. Think about the impact of a child's getting good grades and where that takes him or her in life. Perhaps to college, or on the way to a dream profession? The most important fact to remember about expectations is that the approach means everything:

❑   Expectation is a tool, not an abstract idea.

- ❑ There are two ways to approach the tool, either through faith or fear. Both create a self-fulfilling prophecy.

- ❑ Rooting expectations through faith creates a sense of positivity and a greater likelihood of success. It also allows creativity to flourish.

- ❑ Fearful expectations often lead to inaction and negativity. It crushes creativity because it paralyzes the mind.

- ❑ Diminished expectations have the same effect— "Diminished expectations are a sword through the heart."

- ❑ Combine faith with open-mindedness because learning more helps expectations materialize into results.

- ❑ Creativity nurtures expectations and vice versa. You can learn to become more creative!

When thinking about the meaning of expectations, key words to remember are faith and fear, open-mindedness, and creativity. It sounds like expectations are what you need in your life, right? Understand what goes into expectations, eliminate fear, and your faith and open-mindedness will create new results you never imagined possible.

Chapter 3

Harnessing Expectations and Creating Passion

The greatest expectation I have ever experienced in life was the birth of my children! It was a prayer answered from childhood. I had the distinct honor of witnessing the birth of all three of my children. Though I have witnessed all kinds of births, nothing compares to the birth of our own creation, conceived in love and passion through the grace of the almighty God above. I have said and believed that God's gift to man is woman, and God's gift to man and woman is their children. As with every good thing in life, God's gifts are never to be disrespected or dishonored, ever! All I can say to any young man reading this is "Don't ever miss the opportunity to see the birth of your child. It's life changing and you will have a greater appreciation of the gift of life that has been granted and entrusted to you from God above." It will tie the knots that complete your existence on earth.

For me it was easy to expect fatherhood to be a joyous, life-changing role in life. I am passionate about family and expected that the change a child brings, and the workload along with it, would be worth it even if times weren't smooth and simple. By funneling the expectation that "it wouldn't always be easy, but worth it" into the hardest but most rewarding job that life has to offer, my passion for it bred positivity, which begot more positivity.

The way that I've approached expectations is with a positive attitude. The way I've created a passion for life is that I'm committed to stretching my thinking. When I set and hold close to expectations, I recognize that they are ever-changing. Accepting that is one of the keys of expectation therapy. Expectations are not simply something we understand—we must *do* something with them each and every day! We have to set realistic expectations that we adjust on a moment-by-moment basis because a situation can change so fast. My expectations are what drive everything in me, and I'm beginning to see that's what makes me different from many other people.

One way that I've harnessed my expectations is to be realistic with them, to keep them in focus and in control, and to make sure that they are ever changing to be compatible with the situations that I'm in. Because I'm a big problem-solver, that quality becomes a way for me to not only adjust and think about my expectations, but to understand and *expect* that every problem can be solved.

In fact, I'd wager that we could solve any problem in this world with communication and creative thought. Creative problem solving is educational, personal, and societal, and its use spans every facet of life. Think about it! Teachers wonder how to best teach kids certain material. We use creative problem solving in our relationships when times are tough. Politicians create new solutions to existing problems (sometimes). By understanding the importance and versatility of problem-solving skills, and understanding the way that I think about them, I am adjusting and changing my expectations based on the situation and the information that I'm processing in my mind at that time.

Expectations and therefore success are more attainable when people keep goals realistic. They also have to keep them changing, they have to have short-term expectations and long-term expectations, and they have to adjust to the outcome, all the events leading up to it, and the process. Of course, it goes back to expectations being based *not* on what people expect of you—although those clearly do exist and have their place—but the most important expectations are those you yourself create in your mind for yourself.

Dr. Jim Taylor discusses expectations as key for parents to help their kids through early development. He talks about two expectations we should absolutely avoid (and I fully agree):

1. Expectations based on ability
2. Expectations that are based on a desired outcome.

Ability expectations are harmful because, as you'd expect, they depend on a child's ability—something he or she has no control over due to their genetic predispositions. When the child does not succeed and meet the expectations, it leads the child to "fail" based on something out of their control. Imagine a child having to pass a standardized test on history when he or she is not a rote memorization type of person, as myself. If that child was taught in only one way, one that favors memorization, then the expectation is harmful. It does not match with his or her ability!

Outcome expectations, on the other hand, might be something as simple as a father telling his son to "Go out and win that football game!" The parent puts the burden on that child with what can often be an unrealistic expectation. The problem with outcome expectations is that they are black and white—you either win or you don't. So the chance of failure is high. Additionally, the football-playing son may have all the ability in the world to do just that and win the game, but because he is expected to, the parent has put an undue amount of stress on him by predicting or wanting a certain outcome for him. The psychological makeup of the child is not favorable for optimal results.

Dr. Taylor then brings us to the ideal scenario for expectations: the *effort-based expectation*, where you encourage the efforts of a child rather than his ability or outcome. When I look back on my life I can acknowledge that his assertion is so true. All my life I've had a strong work ethic, which I believe has increased my ability to reach my expected results. When we think back to the fact that expectations need to be realistic and that every problem can be solved with creative effort—mental and physical effort—Dr. Taylor's article only reinforces the idea. His hypothesis makes sense and melds with my methodology. We as parents are the ones who set expectations for our children's lives and help set them on a path to create their own expectations.

Then the question arises in my mind: where and how did I learn this ideology for myself? My parents didn't set goals or expectations, though they may have internalized them without expressing them verbally to me. However, that returns me to my rule: if you don't express it, how can anything come to fruition? For me it would've helped if my parents had stated or written down goals and expectations. They didn't. The "how" of getting past my upbringing is thanks to my Marine Corps experience. I know it's the way that I've trained myself to think.

Effort-based expectations are applicable and teachable to both adults and children. By teaching adults and children these effort-based expectations they become more of a way of life, or habits. When we focus on effort as a means for results, it creates excitement and creativity. It goes back to Pavlov rewarding his dog, ringing a bell and giving the dog a treat; there are immediate rewards when we see our efforts growing and changing the status quo. We can see development right away and feel good about ourselves. It builds that confidence, that "can do" attitude we need. We need the creative thinking that comes from it; we need the discipline that comes with it.

Dr. Taylor warns that a focus on results can trigger undue pressure on a child (or anyone else). This in turn inhibits performance and gives a higher likelihood for missing the mark. When we place special emphasis on the effort, the ability to flourish in an endeavor increases:

> By focusing on the process rather than the outcome, your children will more likely perform better and, if they perform better, they're more likely to achieve the outcome you wanted in the first place.

As the saying goes, it is about the journey, not just the destination. Becoming aware of this and funneling our energy into that will create an optimal psychological environment for success. Again—expectations create a self-fulfilling prophecy!

All in all, whether we like it or not, delivering results is how our world works. Results are how we build a better future, so we cannot ignore them. If we keep pushing our expectations and use them to motivate ourselves, we can all start to see the pay-off in results—and mind you, it might be an unrealistic expectation to think that way—but when the majority does this, it becomes beneficial for everyone. We've talked about creating anxiety in ourselves by creating unrealistic expectations. However, the beauty of focusing on effort is that we don't create anxiety and we don't create the idea that it's difficult. Effort-based expectations keep endeavors positive and drive creativity. The way the world is going to solve the most difficult problems is by people creatively solving them. It all lends itself to the idea of effort-based expectations.

MOTIVATION VS. PASSION

Have you ever watched a YouTube video or read a blog and thought, *I'd sure like to meet this person*? I think this all the time because I love connecting with people because I learn so much from interaction—the eye contact, touch, and inflections in their voice add so much to a conversation. Whenever I meet someone I learn so much just by their movements and eye contact.

My cousin in Fort Worth shared a video on Facebook recently, which reinforced this passion of mine. A couple filling up their car at a gas station encounter a newsman on the monitor of the gas pump. The newsman asks him if he can sing, and if he could, the station would pay for the gas. After asking a few questions regarding song selection, the man (whose name is Will) breaks out into a passionate rendition of Bon Jovi's "Livin' on a Prayer."

My point is that this couple clearly enjoyed life, treasured each moment, and made the most of anything. These are the kind of people whom I find so interesting— those living life with joy in their hearts and spirits. Hats off to you, Will and his wife. You're the kind of people who make this world so great! You have such expressive faces, smiles, and gestures that ignite good will across the earth. I appreciate the hope and spirit that the couple spread, but most importantly, their clear passion for singing and living.

Motivation and passion are both central to expectations because they are the fuel to the fire, powering us to meet our expectations. While they sound similar—they are both positive and drive action, after all—there is a fundamental, huge difference between them. Motivation can be instilled by many sources such as books, speeches, movies, etc. Any of the above can provide motivation when we're lacking it. Passion and self-motivation, however, come from within. We develop it based on our personal expectations in all phases of our lives. So when we expect to be motivated at a lecture, it usually happens on a short-term basis, but when we're passionate about something, it comes from within. It takes little effort to be passionate about something because of how it's integrated in the mind, heart, and soul. To become motivated about something is relatively easy. We often hear people say, "What do I have to do to get you motivated about this?" We rarely hear, "How do I get you passionate about something?"

Take my feelings about expectations. Expectations have been burned in my heart and soul for so long. I am fueled by my passion for the topic, which helps to get my flurry of thoughts organized. This is part of knowing and working with our passions directing them to become fruitful, teachable ideas for anybody to institute.

In short, that's the difference between passion and motivation. Motivation is instilled, while passion is innate. We must continue to develop our passions within ourselves over time.

Does that mean passion cannot be learned?

Of course not! It's not unusual for motivation to ignite passion over time. But there are even more specific guidelines for making it happen.

HOW TO GENERATE PASSION

The Tea Time eBook *Life Lessons: How to Develop a Life You Truly Have a Passion For* is an eye-opening guide to learning the art of passion and how to apply it to life. From the book I've gleaned helpful information to set anyone on a path to passion. My understanding of its guide to the development of passion is below:

- ❑ Attend to yourself: it's similar to shower epiphanies
- ❑ Channel your childhood

- ❑ Gain others' input
- ❑ Notice recurring themes
- ❑ Dabble in uncommitted ventures
- ❑ Jump in!

I often have my great ideas in the shower. There's something about the mindlessness of tending to my hygienic habits—the rhythmic, circular motions of lathering shampoo—that allows for mind*ful*ness. Surely you've had some shower epiphanies, too! The same idea goes for working out, shopping alone, or any activity that allows you to become introspective. Those moments are vital.

Another great way to find passion is to channel childhood. Did you ever color for endless hours? Did you like to put on puppet shows? Return to those childhood fancies and rethink them. Maybe you're a natural artist and have forgotten. On that note, ask what others remember about that time in your life. Don't be afraid to seek help. Pay attention to life—and maybe you'll see those fancies return.

Sometimes it also helps to develop these passions by diving into uncommitted ventures. By "uncommitted," I mean it in a nonprofessional sense. Maybe volunteer, join an organization for the betterment of that passion, and so on. Take a makeup course, if your heart tells you to. Whatever you do, dive into it wholeheartedly and, of course, without hesitation.

NEVER UNDERESTIMATE FENG SHUI

Remember that your surroundings play a huge role as you discover and develop passions. Face it: certain places are more conducive to that than others. Maybe you have to come realize you want to write. You wouldn't want to give writing a test run in the middle of a televised football game with the volume high and people cheering on your couch. Go to a coffee shop and let the caffeine stimulate your mind and the soothing jazz music wash over you. Of course, everyone is different. Just pay special attention to your needs and it will be much easier to run with your passion.

∽

Sometimes, even when we take the measures I listed in bullet points, passion still eludes us. It is okay to explore. Try new things without fear! There is a saying: "Never a failure, always a lesson," and it is something to take to heart. With this, your expectations do not plummet. Go in expecting to learn something new, and you'll come out more confident even if you were outside of your comfort zone.

FINDING PASSION IN THE MUNDANE

Another way to discover passion is to simply look around you at this very second in time. Sometimes we take life for granted. We get into a routine, or we have pressing responsibilities to take care of at work, at school, at home—you name it. It's too easy to forget the beauty of the scene before us. As Lao Tzu said:

"If you are depressed you are living in the past. If you are anxious you are living in the future. If you are at peace you are living in the present."

Be here now. Examine the task you are doing. How can you make it more interesting? Pay attention to some aspect of it you never noticed before. Do something differently. Fine tune your actions. Write a list of your expectations for that activity. Make goals to meet to keep you invested and interested.

Do something with other people. Make sure they are positive, as positivity is contagious. It will infuse new zeal into any task. There are so many of these spirits moving through our lives, far too many to list. We each have our own guiding forces that inspire us; we just have to be receptive to people and learn from whatever they have to offer. It doesn't matter if it's at work, home, or school, be receptive to the message and devour it (which, of course, augments your passion). We all can learn so much from Will, the singer at the gas station: Live without fear, smile like the whole world is watching, and sing like there is no one watching!

In sum, simply paying attention and finding new ways to do a task will reenergize any activity. Get lost in your work and have fun. Most importantly, people have the ability to inspire you and plant a seed of passion because passion is contagious (Tea Time eBooks, 2013).

THE MANY EXPLANATIONS FOR MOTIVATION

Both motivation and passion play a valuable role in helping expectations come to fruition, although they are fundamentally different, as we discussed. But because motivation is a way to get us going in pursuing a behavior or a course of action, it's important to stop and think about this piece of the puzzle. How exactly does motivation fuel us to make expectations a reality?

Susan Krauss Whitbourne, in a 2011 article titled "Motivation: The Why's of Behavior," outlines various hypotheses to explain how motivation generates behavior.

❑ Instinct Theory: We do what we do because of "biologically pre-programmed instinctual urges." Behavior is the result of our wiring.

❑ Drive Reduction Theory: We are driven toward balance, which is the state in which all our needs are fulfilled.

❑ Arousal Theory: We seek to increase our level of stimulation. It's at the opposite end of the spectrum from homeostasis. We seek the high, the rush of endorphins, after pushing ourselves physically and mentally. Whitbourne reminds us "Too much arousal can also thwart our ability to achieve our goals." She tells us to think of Goldilocks and the three bears. Each individual has "its own peak between arousal that is too low and arousal that is too intense." We each have an optimal level to meet.

❑ Incentive Theory: For example, you decide that you will work out every day this week so you can enjoy a pint of Ben & Jerry's, guilt-free, on Saturday night. "You expect that by having this 'thing,' you will be better off than you are without it" (Beckmann & Heckhausen, 2008). That's why we find so many goodies, like chap sticks, gum, and candy bars near the checkout line at the grocery store.

❑ Cognitive Theory: Whitbourne explains that this theory "proposes that our expectations guide our behavior. You'll behave in ways that you think will produce a desirable outcome." Further, there are two categories of motivation:

- *Intrinsic*: Intrinsic motivation drives us to fulfill our inner potential and interests. The desired outcome is to meet our true self in our behavior.

- *Extrinsic:* Tangible rewards are in the outcome.

❑ Self-Determination Theory: With this there's a combination of intrinsic and extrinsic motivation. Motivation comes from feeling in control. A sense of autonomy endows you with self-direction, which leads to satisfaction.

❑ Self-Actualization Theory: Reaching our inner potential drives us. According to Abraham Maslow, it's not about reaching perfection, but continually engaging in a process of "becoming."

It's important to note that our motivations are fluid depending on our physical, financial, and emotional states in life. Think of Maslow's pyramid of needs.

Maslow's Hierarchy of Needs

We need to meet basic physiological needs—food, water, excretion, and so on—before we can move on to attain high-order needs. What motivates us will be more animalistic at the lower levels; if we are not able to find food, our motivations are clear and simple. If we're not getting what we need to survive, we do not feel safe. Likewise, if we reach the second level in Maslow's Hierarchy (safety and security, etc.), then how can we be motivated to fulfill our needs for creativity? It is similar to passion and goes back to the importance of our surroundings in breeding it. If we are not in a safe environment, it's difficult to become motivated.

WHEN PEOPLE USE NEGATIVE EXPECTATIONS: COLLECTIVE DIMINISHED EXPECTATIONS

Recently I was at an Independence Day function, and some of the people there hadn't seen me in several years. "What are you up to these days, Art?" one person asked.

"I'm working on a book about expectations," I replied.

The first words that came out of this person's mouth were "One of my favorite quotes is 'Don't expect anything and you'll never get hurt.'"

I replied that it was actually one of my least favorite quotes on expectations because it operates on the principle of diminished expectations, which, I explained, is one of the ways people are controlled. I went on to assert that I believed expectations are the center of all learning and creativity.

Head cocked, this person said, "Why, I hadn't even thought of it that way!"

That's something I hear quite often. The point at which I'm arriving is that in our world, country, and society, we have gotten to a point where we take expectations for granted and are even oblivious to them. It's something that happens so much because we have so many expectations. We lose sight of what the word "expect" really means and what living an expectant life means. We take it all for granted, to the point that we just fall into the standard way that the media, government, churches, and everyone wants us to think—to want less for our lives and to avoid rocking the boat, causing any waves, and challenging anything... and it is the way creative thought is stymied.

Everything I'm saying here goes back to a term I've devised called *collective diminished expectations* and its use as a control mechanism. It explains the phenomenon by which governments, religions, or any group or person who wants to control a group of people starts convincing others that if they don't expect anything, then they won't be affected by it and it won't bother them. How do we subvert collective diminished expectations and their negative hold over society? By changing our way of thinking about expectations in our culture. We must heighten our expectations! If we don't, expectations will continue to diminish further and further until they retain little of their true meaning and function.

That July 4th conversation reminded me of the negativity swirling around the word "expectations" with opinions such as, "I don't want anything expected of me!" I've heard the negative part of it so much that after I start talking to people, they change their minds and shift their perspective, beginning to realize that it's not about what others expect of them. Instead, it's what they as individuals expect of themselves that matters the most. Thinking *I don't expect much* or *we don't expect much of our kids' church*, and *I certainly don't expect anything of my government* all fall into the trap of diminished expectations. More than anything else in this country, we need higher expectations across all levels of society.

While I don't want to focus on negative expectations, there are a few details worth pointing out. One is how negative expectations affect our world, how we look at them, and how they affect kids and youth. If you type "expectations" into Google and look in the images or any of the document files, you'll find an overwhelming voicing of negative expectations. There are tons of comments saying something to the effect of "Don't expect anything from anybody or you'll get hurt."

One of the quotes supporting that is from a Leo Babauta article from the Zen Habits website titled "Toss Your Expectations into the Ocean":"When reality doesn't meet our fantasy, we wish the world were different." This inequality between reality and fantasy creates a sense of discontentment, which could have been avoided had we not "forced people into the containers [we] have for them" and instead started "seeing things as they are."

I started putting some thought into it and realized it falls into the category of collective diminished expectations. It is probably one of the biggest lies perpetrated on mankind. By now we are familiar with my belief: positive begets positive, negative begets negative. When we start destroying the creativity of people, problems are not solved.

One of the biggest examples of this in America right now is that we're in a huge power struggle between the far left and far right of politics. That's really all it is: a power struggle. Neither party is at fault even though each side claims that the other party is the problem. The reality of the conflict is that both political parties, Democrats and Republicans, perpetuate this struggle. That way they control people, the masses, by inciting them to disagree. As we all know, issues that we should be solving are not getting resolved because the power struggle between the left and the right continues each day. I believe the vast majority of people lie somewhere between the far right and the far left. The problem is they are controlled by these two groups and are at opposite ends of the spectrum and think it's either one group's way or the other's—that the voices of the majority do not matter. We have been going through this ever since governments and groups of people formed. What politics does is, as Philip II of Macedonia said in the 4th century B.C., "Divide and conquer."

Through collective diminished expectations, the message in politics, in any aspect of life, becomes:

"Don't expect anything from anybody."

"Don't get hurt."

"Don't expect anything from the government because they won't do anything."

"Don't expect anything from the education system because it's the parents' job."

We have a game of tug-of-war going on! That's what diminished collective expectations are about. It is the wedge driven in by the media, through the school system, and prevalent just about anywhere. Think about it! The only way we are ever going to get beyond collective diminished expectations is by having *higher* expectations, expecting *more* of government, but particularly expecting more of *ourselves*, because everything starts with the individual. We are never going to solve the problems in this country unless we expect more. We should expect more of ourselves, our school systems, our governments, our employers (who in turn expect more of their employees), and everyone else.

There is talk about cutting government funding right now, and it shows how diminished collective expectations are manipulated to achieve results. Think about one complaint about the government—perhaps you think it is inefficient, for example. How could we make government efficient? By changing the culture of the employees in government and how they represent the institution. We created this massive conglomerate called government, and it is out of control. Everybody knows government is out of control with spending, yet we do little to resolve it. Instead, we keep spending and spending. A businessman knows if he spends more than he takes in on a yearly basis, his business will not survive.

To put it short and sweet, the whole premise of this example is that government is inefficient, yet we do very little about it as its citizens. We have collective diminished expectations telling us that it cannot be solved. It *can* be solved if we put our heads together! Sometimes it's hard to recognize collective diminished expectations because they are so subliminal and done in small, incremental stages over a long period of time. People don't even realize their expectations are lowering. Collective diminished expectations are typically done so covertly over time that we have gotten to the point where we don't expect anything from anyone and poisonous thoughts settle in our minds…

Don't expect anything from yourself, don't expect anything from parents, don't expect anything from teachers, don't expect anything from clergy, and don't expect anything from government officials.

It's sickening because we should expect more and more, but they have us thinking less. With expectations, we get what we ask for. We get exactly what we expect, so we continue getting little from the government or anybody we expect little from. Until we turn around our expectations and seek higher returns, it is going to continue to deteriorate in this country. We need to change it by thinking about what each of us can do to expect more of others. Think on a smaller scale, and it can easily go up from there. Sign an online petition supporting your case and email it to others. Make a phone call. Engage others in dialogue. Simply ask questions!

Actions start with the individual. The answer lies within us alone.

DON'T ABANDON EXPECTATIONS; EXPECT THE UNEXPECTED!

Life is full of many ups and downs, moments of inconceivable joy, tremendous suffering, and utter boredom, yet in the end it is all part of a beautiful ride.

We are blessed to have a conscious mind, but it has also been one of our greatest enemies. Because of how our minds are hard-wired, we perceive the world in a way that keeps us from actually experiencing it in its totality. Think about it: our minds function through memory and logic, and even if we are crazy, the way in which we think may still seem logical to us. We all live with a little censor that resides inside us and is constantly comparing every experience and interaction we've ever had, and this comparing inevitably leads us to have many expectations.

What is an expectation? An expectation is a logical or not-so-logical way in which we want the events of our lives to unfold and how we think things should be, based upon the experiences we have had in the past. We look out into the world through filters influenced from the millions of impressions we have accumulated, all safely tucked away in our brains.

Having expectations automatically makes an ideal in our mind a destination, although it is not yet real. When our minds become closed and function on conclusions, we cease to learn from the events of our lives. But through willpower and effort, many of us achieve some of our expectations.

On the surface this may seem great, but I question whether this is *really* the most joyous way to live our lives. Are expectations necessary? Shouldn't life be lived simply and not made extraordinarily complicated?

If you answered the above with "Then maybe I should get rid of expectations," answer me this: How do we even live a life without expectations?

The first step to living life with expectations without becoming stressed out is to become aware of our inner censors, or the little voice inside us that automatically begins to evaluate and compare any situation against the backdrop of our beliefs. Then, based on the resulting evaluation, which is always incomplete, we will proceed with some type of action or non-action (though the latter is still a form of action).

Once we see the little voice in operation, we become aware of it and identify with it, buy into it—or remain a passive, unattached witness to it. Eventually we see that this may not necessarily be the best way for us to respond to a situation. This goes back to being open-minded in Chapter 2. Don't become identified with that little voice. Instead, learn to constantly question your little inner voice. *By doing that we automatically create inner space for us to freely observe our thinking processes.*

It's easy to initially decide to witness our mind, but it is extremely difficult to remain unidentified. If I ask you to take a minute to watch your mind right now—passively, remaining unattached, yet very attentive—then you may see that you can do it for a short while, but how long can you remain in this attentive state? This will show you that we are often on automatic during the day because the majority of our time is spent inattentive.

This is why things "just happen" in our lives without clear cause. We really don't *do* anything. If we make a strong, determined resolution to do something, but soon become inattentive and situations and events ensue, then we rationalize why things did not work out the way we expected them to.

There is a place in our resting consciousness that allows time to be totally free of expectation in solitude and peacefulness. The Dalai Lama once said, "I am open to the guidance of synchronicity, and do not let expectations hinder my path." If you are able to remain unidentified, switch your awareness to your body and all the subtle, nonverbal communication that it gives, you will be able to separate your body and your mind. Your body has intelligence that functions in present time; therefore, it has no expectations about the future.

Sure, many times these signals may seem illogical, but you have to remember that this is life's very nature.

Life unfolds in miraculous ways the moment you embrace it; you expect the unexpected unexpectedly. Every day is an opportunity to learn something new.

For many of us to make this jump, the requirement is to attune to different aspects of our being. Our organism has been corrupted, become dull, and does not function in top shape. We need to learn to let our mind do its job of sane, rational thinking, and our heart's job of feeling, without allowing our logic and emotion to spill into each other and become corrupted. We need to learn to avoid becoming identified with negative emotions (and refuse to express them). We will see why if we work on this, yet this is the most difficult idea to put into practice. Each of us must make sure we take great care of our individual bodies so that they are sensitive, so their intuitive and instinctual perceptions are allowed to function.

When we are in harmony, we are able to process our expectation of how life should be and be fully available to what life actually is. See where life takes you. Enjoy the ride.

Sure, it makes logical sense to make definite and specific plans and to achieve those plans, but for me life is more fulfilling when it is approached with positive expectations. Expectations are by definition based on the future, not on prior events and thought patterns. Maintain a curious attitude, like that of a child with eyes filled with wonder, desiring to explore a world that is unknown to him or her.

Live life, instead of obsessing over how to best do it. The tag line from Leo Babauta's blog says, "Smile, breathe, and go slowly." That pretty much sums it up.

WHAT DO MEDITATION, PRAYER, AND EXPECTATIONS HAVE IN COMMON?

Have you ever been to a sporting event or a large group meeting where you can feel the energy flowing through the stadium or room? The energy is palpable and spreads to you, pumping you up.

For example, you are at a football stadium and the home team is down by twenty-one points. The home fans are dejected and sense imminent loss. But their coach and team on the sidelines are full of hope and believe that they can still pull it off and win. The coach pulls his quarterback aside and lets him know that he believes in him, he can master the victory, and he can be the hero! After the pep talk the quarterback heads back out onto the field for the next series of downs and hands the ball off to the running back. Lo and behold, he picks up twelve yards and a first down. All of a sudden the faint belief that they can win starts growing with the crowd's positive energy. The home crowd stands and starts cheering them on. Their belief explodes, the momentum swings, the other team starts to doubt, and there you have it—victory!

What has happened is that the home team's belief and expectations rose to a level that caused the atmosphere of the stadium to change in a positive way. At the same time the atmosphere of the away team dropped and diminished;

self-doubt crept in and changed the outcome of the game. It's not the only factor but it is the major factor. Lots of skills and abilities have to be in congruence to make this happen.

Some folks in the stands may have been praying and some may have been meditating. The one thing in common is that the focus and attention were on the outcome of victory. When we collectively focus on outcomes, both good and bad, they often come to pass. It matters what you think, and the effort you put into thinking a thought reflects in the results!

Another example that comes to my mind is Mohammad Ali. When he was a young fighter he would boast," I am the greatest." The whole nation started using this phrase to describe him. We don't have to guess the outcome since history has proven Ali to be correct. He went go on to become the greatest fighter of all time.

Believe and put forth the effort, and it will likely come to pass. It has been shown over and over again, time after time.

How do meditation and prayer work into the equation of success and failure? It lies in the effort that is put forth. When we mentally focus our attention on something, we begin to move in that direction. There is a fine line between prayer and meditation; it is a matter of the effort that is put into it. Meditation is a focusing of the mind, clearing of thoughts, and construction of a pathway to clarity. Prayer is a focusing of thoughts and communication with God. The keys to prayer and meditation are effort and focus. The more focus and effort we put into the act, the greater the results. This is the common thread in all that we endeavor to accomplish. It is my belief that when we focus on things, we are actually changing the patterns of molecules in either a positive or a negative manner, which results in a change of direction of movement, thoughts, and events. This is a powerful process when you stop and put it into perspective. It means we hold the power to change the course of events.

Where it has to begin is in our individual belief systems. We have to be the source and then live it out in effort; the actions then allow for the expectations to take hold and become contagious. When prayer, meditation, and expectation levels are raised and effort is put into developing them, the results can and will be life-changing. In contrast, if we do not, then we float along in discord with our environment and ourselves. The common threads to prayer, meditation, and expectations are the effort and focus that drive our self-fulfilling prophecies.

CONCLUSION

So, I challenge each of us to not eradicate expectations altogether, but to find a way to update them. Updating and managing expectations, even funneling them for our own purposes, is how we harness them. Were our expectations realistic? Can they be altered? Did we learn something from the experience that will help us meet our goals next time? That's what we need to focus on—evaluating our expectations on a moment-by-moment basis in order to ensure we get the results we desire. If you're jaded by past experiences, don't let yourself fall into regret or resignation. After all, "You cannot change what has already been handed to you, but you can absolutely find a positive course of action" (Marston, 2012). The past can either function as shackles in your life, holding you back from a bright future, or it can become a learning experience from which you bounce to the next opportunity, endowed with a greater sense of wisdom.

In review:

- ❏ We can better harness our expectations by infusing positivity and passion into them.

- ❏ To best ensure our expectations are met, we must do something with them every day—often through adjustment and evaluation of the situation and the information on hand.

- ❏ Expect to solve problems by bringing your creativity to them.

- ❏ In parenting, there are two types of expectations we shouldn't use: ability expectations and outcome expectations.

❑ Expectations should be based in effort. It's about the journey, not the destination. We gain life skills from setting expectations.

❑ Effort-based expectations are driven by motivation and passion.

❑ Contrary to popular belief, passion can be learned.

❑ There are many theories for motivation, but our motivations depend on our physical and emotional states (Maslow's Hierarchy of Needs).

❑ People can aggregate their individual negative expectations into collective diminished expectations. We can eliminate them through *higher, positive* expectations.

❑ Sometimes it's more stress-free and fruitful to focus on how to implement expectations instead of the expectations themselves.

❑ We *harness* expectations to change events.

Chapter 4

Setting the Most Important Expectations: Self-Expectations!

"Whether you think you can or think you can't, you're right."

—*Henry Ford*

Are you just floating through life, unclear about what to do next? Chances are that you are suffering from the lack of expectations. You can and will find your way if you so choose. How? You ask. Because all you have to do is want it. It begins with you.

Expectations all begin with an individual. While it's important to have expectations for others, the most important expectations we have are for ourselves. It determines the outcome of a situation before it even transpires! Here we will discuss the key elements in developing self-expectations—and these expectations are useful not only for marriage and parenting, but also in occupations, sports, and religion. They are applicable across the spectrum of life, so it's easy to make this work for us in some facet or another. To develop expectations for ourselves that will stick and give us results, we must simply:

1. Identify expectations through honest contemplation.
2. Write them down!
3. Commit them to memory.
4. Infuse effort into making the expectations happen.

One of the first things to do in order to develop lasting expectations for ourselves and get results is to identify the outcome (expectation) we want, of course. To do this we need to dig deep into our heart, soul, and mind, and spend some contemplative time to get to the root of what we want in our lives. This involves visualization from dreams about what we want to do. The key element in identification of our expectations is being brutally honest with ourselves in finding our passions and what we want to do. Be introspective and candid! Do you want to be a writer but have little experience? Never mind that for now, just don't stifle the dream in the back of your brain any more. Let it shine as a beacon to guide your expectations. You'll find a way there.

Number two is to simply write them down and outline a plan of action. There is so much documentation out there about the benefits of writing down goals and expectations.

Set realistic timetables. Create a vision board. Essentially, anything we write down or put to paper and focus upon comes to fruition. Every class I've ever been to regarding realizing something we want is about writing it down and putting it in view—on the refrigerator, on the computer, as a screensaver, and so on. All of those ideas keep the expectations in front of us so we can visualize them and believe that they are possible. Have you ever written a list of healthy foods or posted a picture of yourself at your thinnest on the fridge for some inspiration? That's the idea. Once we have written them down and identified the expectations, then you can start to build your belief system because expectations are based upon it—i.e., fear versus faith. Whether faith or fear, it's all part of our belief system, our foundation. It's amazing how much we have the power to create when we believe.

Last, commit the expectations to memory and keep them rolling through the thought process. We must keep expectations in the forefront of our minds all the time. It becomes a sort of integrity, something we do daily as a habit. Research has shown that if we do something for twenty consecutive days, and commit our mind to do it throughout each day, after twenty days it becomes a habit. If you want to stop biting your nails, for example, then put a reminder in a place you will see it. If you tend to bite your nails when your job gets stressful, make a noticeable note on the desk. Keep a calendar handy so you can count down the twenty days. Then it should be ingrained in you—no biting your nails!

The most important part of any plan to make something happen is taking action! We can dream it, think it, and play around with it, but it has little chance of happening until we actually put it into action and start doing it, getting it going without hesitation or procrastination, infusing passion into the action!

What if you don't have a clue what your expectations are and what they should be? Here is what I suggest you do:

- ❑ Take a little time for yourself and go on a self-discovery journey in your head. Think about what has made you the happiest in your life and what has moved your spirit and heart.

- ❑ Take care of you—diet, exercise, and your mental and physical needs.

- ❑ Seek out others—their ideas, thoughts, and criticism will give you a clearer picture of the true you.

- ❑ Write it all down: goals, thoughts, plans, hopes, and dreams. Writing these down gives you a point of reference and reflection.

- ❑ Step outside of your comfort zone and start living a life that you have designed and planned with expectancy.

If you take a little time and complete these steps, you will start to feel and think in a more positive way about yourself, and you will find your true passions and happiness.

❧

While writing this book, I became interested in quantum physics. One interesting fact I'm learning is that matter is moved together in patterns. I'm beginning to realize that when we start putting our thought patterns together, these thoughts become an electrical impulse that travels into the universe. There is truly a basis for making our expectations happen that way. That's where our belief system comes in: it's another driving force in taking action because it gets everything moving. Once our plan gets moving, a rippling effect ensues—the butterfly effect is a prime example of this. It stretches across the universe as a contagion. I wish I could imagine an entire world with high expectations. The creativity would be unbelievable. We wouldn't have a tenth of the problems we have if we just put our creative minds to work and thought of our minds as boundless. Once we remove the boundaries of the mind, its reach is limitless and we have the power to do anything. We just have to put our thoughts into action!

In a marriage, we can imagine we are going to have the best marriage, and we can go to an endless number of classes and counseling, but until we put effort into our marriage (or into parenting, or any other familial relationship), it's just not going to be as fruitful as we would want it to be. Remember, the effort we put into an event is in direct correlation to the reward we will receive.

For me it comes back to effort. For most of my life I have, thankfully, understood this. It is a value the Marine Corps instilled in me that I'm just coming to realize. They taught me the fearlessness of effort! All my life, I have been able to do new things, and I've darted after a new endeavor fearlessly. Confidently I can say I have no fear of failure. As crazy as it may sound, I experience no fear because I remind myself that there is a learning experience in every opportunity. Whether it's occupation, marriage, sports, or religion, if we put the effort into that facet of our life, we are going to reap the rewards of our efforts.

Consciousness, Emotional Intelligence, Self-Awareness, and Effort

How do we mold these ideas and make them work for us as normal people living our lives every day? First, we need to understand that consciousness and self-awareness are so closely tied together that it's a matter of terminology. We can't be conscious unless we have a certain level of self-awareness, and vice versa. The two are tied together. To explain them, we need to be introspective. That's part of consciousness—when we look at and examine our wants, needs, desires, what we want to accomplish out of life, and what our goals are. Once we do that, we start to realize that it takes in-depth thinking in our conscious mind and then we can move forward.

Being self-aware is also about interacting with people while examining ourselves. When we become self-aware *and* aware of our surroundings, we start to process the world differently. All of this is about how we process things and react to them, what motivates us and drives us forward.

This brings us to the emotional intelligence facet of this discussion: To be intelligent emotionally, we attach definitions to our different experiences, the different feelings, and the different emotions we have. But where change happens is in the effort. We can be conscious and have the emotional intelligence and self-awareness that we want, but unless we do something with it, it means nothing other than increasing our level of self-awareness. In order for emotional intelligence to make a difference in our lives, we have to take it and process these different practices together and move forward in our relationships and in our daily habits. *Everything* is driven by the effort we put into it. As I've said, the effort put in will be the effort that comes out; we get out of it what we put into it.

It's not good enough to be merely knowledgeable. We have to have motivation and effort attached to it to move forward with that newfound knowledge. They are key to everything. In society today, we're at a point where we want things done easily and even want things done for us. I hate to say it, but few people want to work toward improving themselves anymore. They expect it with their sense of entitlement, which is not compatible with being conscious, aware, or anything we mentioned previously. We have to be willing to change ourselves and dig deep inside. We have to decide, "Okay, I've had enough, and I don't want to live like this anymore." Then we go about identifying the situation, working through it, and becoming aware of it. We put forth the effort to change the status quo. It sounds simple, and it is; however, we want to complicate things. It doesn't have to be so muddled. It is so blatantly simple to change if we just identify, accept, and work through the area of necessary change. That's the way it goes.

If you do that, then you can change anything about yourself—and can actually effect change in other people. When they see how you change, it changes how people perceive you, how you perceive people, how people react to you, and how you react to others. Always, for each and every situation, it starts with you. You can create a ripple effect across the universe. The status quo can change! I believe you can solve any problem if you put your mind to it. That's the message I deliver. We're all capable of it. We have to want to do it and put the effort forth to accomplish it.

DON'T HESITATE TO
TOSS HESITATION ASIDE

When we act on expectation with fear instead of faith, hesitation is a common result. When a company hesitates, or a business hesitates, or a teacher, or you or I hesitate, it is a sign of uncertainty in the decision we're about to make. I've trained myself to push through everything fearlessly. Even if I were to make a wrong decision, it is better than hesitating or making no decision at all! In the military, when we hesitate and don't make decisions promptly, devastating effects may follow.

Think of it like this: every hero we hear about today—firemen, policemen, citizens on the street who help people—all of the heroes we talk about have one thing in common: They did not hesitate! They made the effort to save somebody or save an ideal. Heroes come in all forms, all shapes, all religions, and in any way we can imagine. The one thing each and every one of them has in common is that when a situation arises and they make a decision to commit to something, they do not hesitate. They move quickly, efficiently, intentionally, and passionately to help someone in need or help an idea grow. That is the one common factor that they all have. It's a liberating feeling to live without fear and hesitation. We all wonder sometimes how we will react in certain situations. Some of us have had the opportunities because of our occupations or service.

Most of us have not had those experiences, and I pray we are never tested.

But take, for example, Moore, Oklahoma's May 20, 2013 tornados. There are countless unsung heroes in that event alone who did selfless, heroic actions day in and day out. But what made these heroes successful and heroic? The fact is that *they did not hesitate for one minute.* They moved quickly and passionately to save lives or to complete the mission they had. The teachers who mobilized the children to take tornado precautions, the first responders searching through the rubble, and everyone else who was in the danger zone took fast and fearless action—they chose to! Our military does it every day. Our police and firemen and emergency medical technicians members do it every day. Whether they are aware of it or not, one of the fundamental steps in these professions is to abandon fear and to confidently thrust themselves into the situation at hand. To do this involves effort. Even if we make a "bad decision," effort will move us through it to get us back on track to the right decision. So don't waste time; choose something and dive in.

THE HEXAGON OF EXPECTATIONS

There is a cycle that explains what happens when we develop expectations. The Hexagon of Expectations is about the neurological pathway that expectations create in our mind, the process that we use to move through our expectations. It takes two-fifths of a second for an expectation to be processed in our brain. When we follow that hexagon, it takes us through the cycle of how expectations work.

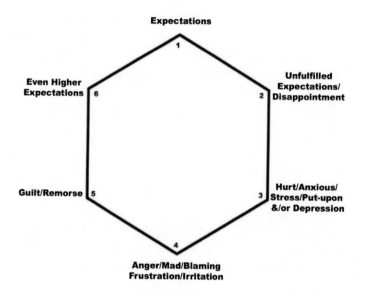

The Hexagon's creator, Charles Brown, says that, "expectations can deliver devastating emotional impact if one's expectations are not managed correctly" (2008). This is why some people come up with the idea of not having expectations at all! But rest assured that with certain maneuvering you can spare yourself the pain and hurt that people fear by having expectations.

Step 1, expectations, turn into Step 2, unfulfilled expectations and disappointment, in the blink of an eye (the aforementioned two-fifths of a second). To conquer the hexagon and avoid Step 2, Brown says we must begin by having realistic expectations. He reminds us to avoid comparing ourselves with others and being "unduly influenced by the expectations of others." We must look at our own current reality and factor it into consideration when we make expectations. Realistic is different from lowered expectations—it's about honesty, which better allows confidence to thrive.

CONCLUSION

Once you figure out what you want your expectations to be, it's simple to get on track to make it happen. After that, you're the commander of yourself. Don't hesitate, just do it!

❑ You can develop expectations and see them through to fruition through contemplation, writing them out, committing them to memory, and putting forth effort.

❑ Still can't identify an expectation? It's time for "you" time. Take a walk and reflect. Write in a journal. Once you're ready, spend time with people you trust and gain feedback.

❑ Believe that you can do it! Belief (faith) is the root of making expectations happen. Don't have fear, because even if you "fail" there's a lesson involved, which is helpful and keeps the endeavor from being a failure at all!

❑ When you put forth effort, you're refusing to heed fear.

❑ Learn self-awareness. Attach meaning to what you learn about yourself (becoming emotionally intelligent).

❑ When you believe in yourself and know a course of action is right, jump into it without hesitation. That way you'll get it done and prove you have faith, not fear.

❑ We can keep ourselves from being sucked into fearful expectations by understanding and mastering the Hexagon of Expectations developed by Charles Brown.

CHAPTER 5

EXPECTATIONS AND OTHERS

Recently there was a great story in Texas about Jeff Bliss, a student who challenged his teacher verbally in class. Evidently her teaching method was to sit behind a desk and pass out packets, and he wouldn't have any of that:

> "You want kids to come in your class? You want them to get excited? You got to come in here and you got to make them excited for this. You want a kid to change and start doing better? You got to touch his frickin' heart" (2013).

He left the room at the teacher's request after giving her a piece of his mind. I think he could have more eloquently stated his position, but what he said was dead-on. After a classmate recorded the argument on video and posted it to YouTube, it went viral, and the community has given Bliss overwhelming support.

To me the video illustrates the important connection between perception and expectation. It can work in two ways, which goes back to faith versus fear. When a community perceives a person as troubled or bad, the stigma stays with them throughout their adolescent years and sometimes all the way through their time in the school system. Their perception may cause them to feel fearful about forming an expectation in favor of a certain outcome.

It could begin with, "Oh, that's John the troublemaker," which quickly becomes sinking sand, a difficult situation from which to break away. Reputations are quickly made and slowly changed. Typically the only way to break out of that is either to leave the environment or wait until they can start afresh. We all hear about the stories of people who did not do well in school but did well in college and beyond. I'm an example. A lot of it was the perception my family had as we spent the years in our new home. We grew up in a small town and were perceived as outsiders. I reacted accordingly when people looked at my family and me as being different, as outsiders they were not very friendly toward. From that point I started acting out in school, which I believe was a reaction to the expectation from the community that we were outsiders. The perception was that I was unlikable and un-included, but I earned the "troublemaker" title by meeting their expectations. This is important to be aware of when we're dealing with adolescents and young people growing up. We must keep an open mind and treat them with understanding—in other words, treat others as we would treat ourselves.

The other part of the perception and expectation connection might be found in the interviews with Jeff Bliss after the video went viral. His mom was a teacher, and my hypothesis is that she probably taught him well at home and his expectations for teachers heightened. When his teacher wasn't meeting his raised expectations for education, he verbalized it to her in no uncertain terms. I do think he could've used more tactful verbiage, but I understand and support his point.

Perception and expectation work both ways. Teachers have perceptions of their students, and their expectations start to meet those perceptions. When students have perceptions of the teacher and/or community, they start to live up to the community's expectations that develop. It's important that we get the two in harmony with each other. A lot of lives are being affected when we give people unfair perceptions which result in diminished expectations—a lot of talent is lost and skill sets that people can use in later life aren't being devoured and made productive.

This phenomenon by which children live up to the expectations of their teachers (or when anybody lives up to another's expectation for them) is called *social labeling*. Quite simply, "People tend to live up to the positive or negative label bestowed upon them" ("The Rule of Expectations: The Impact of Suggestion"). I keep reiterating that expectations are a self-fulfilling prophecy, and this is just one of the many examples of that. Bill Glass once said, "Ninety percent of prison inmates were told by parents while growing up, 'They're going to put you in jail.'" In fact, in inner-city schools, standardized testing is often used to determine the space prisons will need in the future! It does so much more harm than good to think this way. People can perceive others' perceptions of them, and it has a huge effect on their ability to succeed.

For example, if a manager at a retail store constantly berates the employee, saying that they have a lot of work to do, that they aren't doing their job well, then that employee thinks they are doing a terrible job at work. Their insecurity limits them. Productivity plummets because that person believes they are incapable of doing a good job, and they project that and make their low expectations a reality. On the other hand, if that person has a boss or superior who motivates them, expecting better things from them paired with encouragement, then productivity and successful results increase. This is because those who believe in our ability do more than stimulate us. They create for us an atmosphere in which it becomes easier to succeed. We can dig our own grave, or we can scale the heights of our success.

SOCIAL ROLES AND COLLECTIVE DIMINISHED EXPECTATIONS

One quote I've always appreciated is by William Shakespeare: "All the world is a stage, and all the men and women are merely players. They all have their exits and entrances, and one man in his time plays many parts." That is an excellent description of what social roles entail because their influence on others is so strong. Social roles dictate laws and how we behave, because when others expect us to behave a certain way, we either conform or we don't conform. If we choose to not conform, we're called non-conformists—and throughout history, non-conformists have been largely shunned by society. But when we conform, it's part of how rules and behaviors are established. Rules and behaviors are extremely important and have a pronounced effect on each individual culture, country, and part of the world. One phenomenon that has always intrigued me, and thus led me to the construction of a new term, is *collective diminished expectations*, which has a great deal to do with social roles and social expectations.

What Hitler did to the Jews was done through collective diminished expectations. He set up a culture where the Jews were seen as inferior and a threat. Collective diminished expectations were also used to enslave black people; religions have used them to control people. In fact, they're used today in the religious world in many ways, and they're done subtly and incrementally, as I've said, in small phases. Ultimately, they change the pattern of how we think and what we expect. They can be done so gradually over a period of time that we don't realize what is being accomplished.

It would be interesting, although I don't know if it could be proven, if we could determine if the government is consciously doing this practice or if it has been unconsciously developed over the millennia to achieve the goal of controlling people. As far as its relationship to social roles, that's one of its outcomes: control.

Social roles start from infancy and do not stop until we pass away. We have social roles at school; I call them educational social roles. We have relationship roles, from those with our parents to our romantic relationships, which develop into marriage relationship roles. For any social relationship, there's a role. What's more important about the social roles are the collective expectations that drive the results that an employer wants to reach, the school wants to reach, and so on. As I've drilled into you readers, there's nothing that counts more than what you set up in your *own* mind for expectations and how you go about changing your involvement with those roles throughout the history of your life. It sets the stage everywhere you go because it affects your family, the church you attend, your employer...it affects everything. The role of social expectations is huge because it's what sets the stage for how you interact with others in any situation.

It goes back to the old saying, "What you expect of yourself is what counts the most" because it affects others in many different ways. That's one of the basic rules of quantum expectations—there's a ripple effect of actions in relation to the universe (the butterfly effect). That's my take on social expectations and how they affect everything. In the end, take this to heart: What you do affects you and the universe for eons. That's the power of expectations.

MY SUGGESTIONS ON SUGGESTION

Right now in our world, we face more sources of suggestion outside of the family model than ever before because of new technology. We are bombarded with so much information through all types of media—movies, television, books, the Internet—it all adds to the power of suggestion. While swimming through so many external opinions, I can attest to this: because of the way I operate, I spend a lot of time in deep thought to sort through information because I want to use what is prudent and relevant to my set of standards, the lifestyle of my family, and my life. I'm constantly sorting through information and making sense of it. I get to the point where I experience system overload and have to take a step back and relieve myself of the stress and energy that it takes to sort through constant data. That's why I've mentioned that I'm constantly evaluating and thinking through my expectations. At the end of the day I fall asleep immediately because I've worked my mind so much. It's not always a bad thing—the more we work the mind, the more our minds will produce. We will grow our intelligence, emotional intelligence, and all of the faculties that we as human beings use to grow ourselves. That's why it's always a learning experience.

The power of suggestion is vital to growth. We soak in more as children than at any other point in life. As we develop through the different phases of life, we get to the point where we get very good at sorting what we want to take in and what we don't—what suggestions we believe and don't want to believe. We have to stop and think: Who are our influencers? They are of utmost importance because, as the phrase says, "You are who you hang out with." If we hang out with millionaires, we develop a millionaire mentality. If we hang out with gangsters, we gain a gangster mentality. In the educational field with other teachers, we pick up their subliminal expectations and the suggestions they throw out, then we sort through them and develop our own style. To become lifelong learners, hang out with people who have a like mind. Subconsciously, we accept cues from others and act accordingly, making our own expectations. If we use it consciously, it's a persuasive tool. Deciding who or what influences us is extremely important—one of the most important choices we make. Likewise, we must understand that we influence others through our own actions and suggestions.

Throughout my life, I imagined I could be more—no matter what I was doing. One challenge for me was when I had a college professor who wrote "want less" on the board every day. That made no sense to me. Needless to say, I butted heads with him. That is another aspect of collective diminished expectations. He tried to convince us to want less in the sense of physical things, like not wanting Corvettes. Still, the central message disturbed me because any time that we want less, we stop wanting more, which stops intellectual growth, stunts personal development, and breeds fear and hesitation.

We're very susceptible to suggestion, so it only makes sense that those we spend time with will be the source of the majority of our suggestions on how to live life. The question then becomes: Even when the source is a rich vein of suggestions, how do we find our own road to travel? That's the biggest single idea that I want to instill in people. My purpose in life is to let you know that you *can* create more, be more, and don't have to accept the same patterns. In order to do that, start with higher expectations, acting in a fashion that will enhance your achievement of those goals. Then you must elevate yourself in society, education, and employment; that's why it's important that people never give in, conform, and stop trying. This will lead to a successful life.

Remember this: Success isn't necessarily defined by money. Success can be measured by self-fulfillment, awareness, emotional intelligence, and education. I've believed that as long as I had enough to live and take care of the needs of my family and myself, I have been successful. Of course, I didn't stay satisfied with my success and strove to be more—for me, learning new ideas and practices and forming my own points of view are a measure of success, and I don't want to stop learning. In other words, I measure success by growth. For growth's sake, I'm determined to grow in every facet of my life. I don't want to be static; I want to keep accomplishing what I want to accomplish.

I'll end this message with a word of caution: be careful from whom you get your suggestions and how you internalize them. When you listen to another's expectations, it affects the course of your life. You are whom you hang out with. Pick and choose suggestions that are right for you. Move forward, constantly expecting the best that there is each and every moment of the day.

ATTACHMENT, RELATIONSHIPS, AND BONDING: HOW DOES IT AFFECT US THROUGHOUT OUR LIVES?

An article by Jeanne Segal discusses the attachment bond as the path for the first interactive love relationship, the first real relationship that we ever form in our lives. Attachment is responsible for:

- ❏ Shaping the success or failure of future intimate relationships
- ❏ The ability to maintain emotional balance

- ❑ The ability to enjoy being ourselves and to find satisfaction in being with others

- ❑ The ability to rebound from disappointment, discouragement, and misfortune

- ❑ A basis of how to build meaningful relationships with other people (Segal, et al., January 2013)

The lack of the attachment bond creates a phenomenon called *insecure attachment*. It results in marked negativity in your life at a very early age that causes disruption, hesitation, and a decreased sense of overall positivity. It makes people negative often. Relationships aren't as strong, stress isn't managed as well, and isolation and abuse sometimes ensue. It makes sense in some situations where the caregiver hasn't played with or devoted time to the child to create that bond. Something as simple as playtime can help children construct their sense of the world!

What's important and astounding to me is how I overcame my insecure attachment. Granted, I know I was loved as a child and as an infant, but I did not have a strong bond to my mother or my father. My father, who rarely said very much, was an alcoholic. My mother was a workaholic. In the late '40s and '50s, my mother could have been considered a "modern woman" because she owned a business and was driven for success. When we left New Jersey to move to upstate New York, it all changed. For her there were life-altering situations involved that I'm sure I'm not aware of.

No matter the reason, I didn't bond well with my parents. That's why, when I graduated from high school, it was so easy for me to leave, and why I was so eager to leave; I wasn't bonded in the way that my brother and sister were toward my mom and dad. In a way it's tragic, but on a positive note I'm in awe of how I was able to leave the situation I was in. Bonding in another sense had a lot to do with it. I've talked at length about when I was a little boy and walked to the top of the hill and talked to God. The seed of attachment was planted spiritually more than in a familial sense. In my heart and soul, I knew there was something better for me out there. It wasn't where I was at the time, so I chose to move on to the best path I thought available to me—going into the service to better my life and move out of the situation I was in.

It astounds me that I was able to recognize that. I have no clue how I was guided and driven in the way that I was, but I attribute it to my faith rooted in a higher power. No matter what, I expected that there was something better in my life. I just knew it and felt it. That's why I'm so passionate about *Expectation Therapy*. I've linked the experiences of my life and connected them to this endeavor and want to let people know that anything can be overcome when you have faith. Anything. It doesn't matter what it is, you can do it if you follow your positive belief in yourself.

It may sound like I've gotten off track from the attachment bond discussion, but I have not. All the early events in my life contributed to the formation of my thinking, which I now share wholeheartedly. The attachment bond has been a big part of my arrival at these conclusions. I would not be who I am had I not had the feelings of restlessness that I had, wondering what would happen to me and how it would all manifest.

View each event as a huge blessing and learning experience and see where it takes you—even if your attachment is "insecure." Sometimes where life takes you is even more impressive, and remember, "You choose your friends, not your family," as the saying goes. Attachment can be formed elsewhere.

My thoughts to parents: you need to get out and spend time with your children. From their birth to five years old is when children form the social skills that will guide them through their life and motivate them. When they start putting all those skills gleaned from playtime together and create expectations for achievement—whether scholastic, social, or any other category—you have an immeasurably huge impact on how they pursue them and create expectations for any of life's endeavors. We don't have children only to let them be. We must be the guiding light for our children, the light that leads them on a path for excellence and high expectations.

HOW TO COMMUNICATE EXPECTATIONS

Kim Campbell's article on students and expectations is actually the pathway that anyone could use. This is what I hope we will reference as a pathway workbook for kids, adolescents, and adults—really for anyone in any walk of life—to master our expectations. It holds a key ingredient on how to make expectations function. She talks about creating a successful working environment and how expectations are a huge part of that: "To implement high academic expectations, you must first have high expectations for behavior" (Campbell, 2012). It's our life, and expectations are its building blocks! Everything she talks about is really about how our expectations manifest in what we do. She talks about teachers having expectations for students—but really, it translates to anyone.

What does that process entail? Campbell, a 7th-grade teacher, says, "The first rule about expectations is that students must understand what they are, what they mean, and how it looks to meet them." Those are the key ingredients in mastering our expectations. What we have to do is to identify them and translate them into action with a plan. Additionally she discusses having an organizational scheme—skills, procedures, and rules—which are all part of the process of mastering expectations. As she says, if you don't believe in your expectations, who will? That's how you realize and internalize expectations, through self-awareness and self-reflection, to help identify what your expectations are and then move forward. All this creates high behavioral expectations, and academic standards go right into that.

She also discusses having expectations not only for students but also for teachers. It's a two-way street, but it also translates into you and me and everybody involved having high expectations for everybody around us. Think about how there must be expectations for employees—and likewise, expectations for the manager or boss to meet. They must demonstrate competence to serve as a model for what the employees should do. They should be able to mobilize employees and motivate them. If they can't, then that poor leadership has trickle-down effects in the company's performance. It's a cycle: high expectations for leaders result in higher expectations for followers. It also leads to my phrase, "We are who we hang with." I firmly believe that the more good people we surround ourselves with, the better our lives become. Think back to the fact that we take up on cues from others and vice versa. We all affect each other.

Campbell's hypothesis, which I also endorse, is that expectations create *permanent change* in our lives. When we set expectations, we set a routine. As Campbell says, the implementation of expectations creates efficiency and familiarity that keep moving us forward to attain higher goals throughout our lifetimes. When we don't have a clear vision of what our expectations are, we are living more in fear than in faith. Fear starts to create hesitation and misunderstanding, and our expectations begin to lack conformity, creating plenty of problems. That's why writing expectations down and having an action plan are vital. A plan promotes the responsibility and fluidity that make action happen. Lead by example. Set the rules and consequences. Rules have to be short and sweet, and we have to discuss their importance. Once these guidelines are followed, the rules set expectations and these "Clear behavioral and procedural expectations provide the safety that sets minds free to soar" (Campbell, 2012).

That brings us to another key element: communication. If we don't communicate expectations to others, then they don't have any meaning. When we communicate expectations they must also be a) enforceable and b) consistent. Once that occurs, we just have to grab it and run with it, taking action and driving it forward.

In sum, for expectations between people, we must: identify, take action, determine consequences, and create a pathway in our brains for success. If we implement all this, we will move constantly in small increments toward the goals we want. It gets our brain thinking about attainable goals and increases our positivity. That's important because when we display positivity, it's contagious to everybody around us.

CONCLUSION

Our expectations for others (and others' expectations for individuals) have a huge impact on the success of any venture, from school to work.

❑ Perception shapes how people form expectations because other people are huge motivators. If we're viewed as capable, we're more likely to be capable! If we're viewed as incapable, it drags us down and makes us less likely to attain success—basically, the expectations of others impact expectations for ourselves.

❑ Social roles are expectations we're expected to conform to in society. They are the rules governing us in the different "hats" we wear in a variety of situations. They set the stage for expectations in a certain context.

❑ Collective diminished expectations are a way that groups or individuals use lowered expectations to change mindsets for a gain/ulterior motive.

❑ How we perceive ourselves also has an impact on how others see us.

❑ Because our society is bombarded with others' suggestions, it means we have to be aware and evaluate expectations frequently, changing accordingly if need be.

❑ Our sense of attachment affects our expectations for ourselves.

❑ Interaction with children early on impacts how they form expectations of the world and themselves.

❑ In school and in work, expectations are a tool to make success happen across the board. In order to create success, leaders must first communicate expectations and lead by example.

Epilogue

A question that I'm often asked is "Do expectations really matter that much?" My answer is straightforward: "More than you will ever realize." But it goes much deeper when I let my heart's desires run loose with my passion for the need to teach and explore expectations.

Why do they matter? The simple answer is that which we expect equals what we get, or, effort in equals effort out! Expectations are at the core of our intellectual intelligence and drive our human creativity, thought, and actions to move mankind forward both personally and communally. It only makes sense that we have higher expectations if we want to move forward on any level. The problem is the world is moving further and further away from that kind of thinking. My observation is that we seem to be willing to let others do the work and we tend to tag along until it suits us to jump on the bandwagon. This is another way of saying that we have become lazy and are willing to let others take control of the outcome of our lives.

How has this come about? What we have done on a gradual basis is to lower the expectations we have of parents, teachers, community leaders, and ourselves in all facets of our lives. Let someone else worry about it and we'll just live with it. Most people seem happy with that, but at some point the results aren't to their liking or advantage; then the uproar starts and the second-guessing begins.

"How could this have happened?" they ask, pointing the finger at everyone but themselves. Again, this is the easy way out. The question then becomes "How do we change it? Can I really make a difference? Does it really matter in the big scheme of things?"

Change comes in two forms: either it is forced upon us (laws, rules, and legislation) or we make a conscious decision to change our behavior. I feel more comfortable with changing myself by choice versus having change forced upon me. When we have higher expectations in the core of our thought processes and philosophies, then it becomes easier and easier to identify and react to the bombardment of negatives thrown at us throughout our daily routines. I have found it easier to share all my beliefs and passion when I know that my core expectations are of the highest magnitude. You could call it confidence, but all I know is that I'm more comfortable speaking my mind when I know that my core expectations are in the right place. My deepest core expectation lies in faith. Through faith I am assured that all decisions will be as they are intended to be and will work out for the best.

When you find yourself asking if expectations really matter, my hope is that you will take the time to reflect back on your core expectations and answer, "You bet your life they matter, and I've got high expectations." We have lived under the cloud of collective diminished expectations for way too long, and it's driving the performance of the human condition to low levels of apathy. We cannot let this continue or the consequences will be devastating.

∽

What a Bountiful Vision.

I believe that people are inherently good until they prove they aren't, which is much different than what the world teaches—"People have to earn your trust." I believe I surrendered myself to that belief system by becoming fearless. What does that mean?

For one, I have surrendered myself to a higher power. My life's experiences have taught me that I'm a mere speck in the big scheme of things, yet I know that I make a difference in the lives of other people. I also believe that greater things will come to me if I believe, and do I believe? Oh, *yeah*, I do! I believe in the goodness in all living things, friends or foe.

Has my thinking hurt me and have people taken advantage of me?

Yes, but I want to share something my dad once told me. He didn't make a habit of sharing his thoughts, but when he did I was so hungry for his wisdom that it left lifelong impressions. What he told me went like this: "If you trust and give freely with your heart and soul and someone takes advantage of your heart and kindness, then it's not your fault. But shame on them, for they will have to answer for it one day."

Now that I'm older and wiser (older than my father was when he told me this), what a gift it was and what an incredible impact it had in shaping my life's mindset: faith, not fear.

Thank you, Dad, and I love you.

Preview:
Quantum Expectations

I have a deep-seated need to figure things out on my own with little input from outside sources. My process begins with running a concept through my conscience and mulling it over in my mind until I figure out how it came to be, how it connects to other concepts, and what it ultimately means. That process has been no different with my lifelong passion for expectations and their relevance to life as a whole. The journey began when I was a little boy and has brought me sixty-five years later to this point.

I can only imagine what you're thinking—*So what does this have to do with quantum anything*? I'll be making this case in story form, so let's start from the beginning.

There was a little boy who, out of desperation and loneliness, used to climb a hill on his family's farm and look out into the vast universe and wonder what was out there and what he could make of it all. What impact would his life have on the universe? Something spoke to his inner being that kept telling him he mattered, and after many trips up that hill, he started to believe and know the veracity of his importance. He also knew he had to follow the road that lay ahead to find out. He kept believing and following that path no matter where it led him, learning and experimenting at every opportunity, and taking the chance to fully live in the moment that was presented. Some thought he was odd, some thought he was crazy, and some thought he just might have a little bit of brilliance inside of him. He chose to believe those who believed in him.

There were times when the road was tough to travel, and there were times when the path held life's most precious moments, but his faith that there was something huge and special in store for his life didn't falter. He moved forward while maintaining that belief at the core of his mindset and living, learning, and loving all that life placed in his path. Over the years he learned to value people and was inspired by those who crossed paths with him, learning from their experiences.

I guess you're still wondering what in the world this has to do with quantum physics. Well, here are my thoughts: we all have heard stories of people whose thoughts come true after they think them. Many of those have dealt with tragic events that involve death or disaster. Those people think negatively, compounding it to make it worse. I believe that when that little boy put out those positive questions and thought patterns, he set the stage for a life of positive events—a path to follow, or was it an expectation that kicked the wheels into action?

Here's is my hypothesis: when that little boy looked out into that vast universe and asked aloud what was to become of him, he set in motion a sequence of electrical impulses that moved out into the atmosphere and started a chain reaction in the universe, positive charges that rippled across time and space that will continue to have a butterfly effect for an eternity.

Sounds farfetched, doesn't it? But the world of physics and particularly quantum physics is taking huge steps in proving that thought patterns actually send out impulses that can move matter and objects!

It makes sense to me that the mind is a powerful tool and what we think matters in many ways. Expectations are no different. What we expect of ourselves and what we think of ourselves are huge factors in what we make of ourselves and what we become in the course of our lives and those whom we touch.

The fact is that the mind is more powerful than we even know! I seek to prove this hypothesis using quantum mechanical calculations to validate the "expectation value." They have created an equation using that value. Whether that formula can be adapted to theoretical quantum physics or not and what the relationship will be remains to be discovered. In short, the average particle position, the radius of hydrogen electrons at their ground state, their momentum, and energy of free particles may hold the answer to the impact of expectations on our environment—and the universe.

In this book I've mentioned how expectations (or prayer, or meditation) can impact the environment of a football game and eventually determine the outcome. I've mentioned the butterfly effect, and how expectations spread to other people and have lasting consequences through the generations—even seemingly tiny events that resulted from expectations. These ideas all fit into the framework of quantum expectations.

I know it is complicated and intricate thinking, but I am of the belief that there is a scientific basis for the expectations and the impulses we send into the universe. With the help of some pretty smart folks, I think we can prove it. Physics is evolving at a rapid pace, and for the first time there are some theoretical physicists who are starting to change their beliefs about the existence of God. How awesome would that be to have that question answered once and for all?

So there you have it. It's a big question, so I'm thinking it's something we need to cover in the next book!

Bibliography

Babauta, Leo. Zenhabits blog, "Toss Your Expectations into the Ocean." June 29, 2011. Accessed August 23, 2013. http://zenhabits.net/ah/.

Brown, Charles. Grin Therapy—Dr. Boyd Lester: Notes from the Dead Pecker Bench by a Grumpy Old Psychiatrist, "First Thought, Second Thought." Accessed August 23, 2013. http://grintherapy.com/firstthought.html.

Brown, Charles. Grin Therapy—Dr. Boyd Lester: Notes from the Dead Pecker Bench by a Grumpy Old Psychiatrist, "The Hexagon of Expectations." 2008. Accessed August 23, 2013. http://grintherapy.com/hexagon.html.

Campbell, Kim. "Expectations: Do You Have Them? Do Students Get Them?" Adapted from Campbell & Wahl, *If You Can't Manage Them, You Can't Teach Them*. Incentive Publications, 2012. Accessed August 23, 2012. http://www.nassp.org/tabid/3788/default.aspx?topic=Expectations_Do_You_Have_Them_Do_Students_Get_Them

Foster, Wallace. "This Is Water—Full version-David Foster Wallace Commencement Speech." YouTube video, 22:44, posted by "Jamie Sullivan," May 19, 2013. http://www.youtube.com/watch?v=8CrOL-ydFMI.

Marston, Ralph. The Daily Motivator blog, "Keep Expecting the Best." August 2, 2012. Accessed August 23, 2013. http://greatday.com/motivate/120802.html.

McLeod, Saul. Simply Psychology, "Social Roles." 2008. Accessed August 23, 2013. http://www.simply psychology.org/social-roles.html.

Morton, Aaron. Pick the Brain blog, "5 Ways to Become a Creative Powerhouse." May 13, 2013. Accessed August 19, 2013. http://www.pickthebrain.com/ blog/5-ways-to-become-a-creative-powerhouse/.

Mr. Andrews. "Self-Expectations." Accessed August 23, 2013. http://home.earthlink.net/~bmgei/educate/docs/ motivate/expect.htm.

Santos, Joel. Sermon Central, "Expecting the Best." September 2004. Accessed August 23, 2013. http:// www.sermoncentral.com/print_friendly.asp? SermonID=72269.

Segal, Jeanne, and Jaelline Jaffe. HelpGuide.org: A Trusted Non-Profit Resource, "Attachment and Adult Relationships: How the Attachment Bond Shapes Adult Relationships." Last modified May 2013. Accessed August 21, 2013. http://helpguide.org/ mental/eqa_attachment_bond.htm.

Tan, Enoch. Dream Manifesto, "Manifest Desires Freely by Having No Expectations." Last modified August 20, 2007. Accessed August 23, 2013. http://www.dreammanifesto.com/manifest-desires-freely-by-having-no-expectations.html.

Taylor, Jim. Psychology Today, "Parenting: Expectations of Success: Benefit or Burden. Do your expectations help or hurt your child?" Last modified November 4, 2010. Accessed August 23, 2013.

http://www.psychologytoday.com/blog/the-power-prime/201011/parenting-expectations-success-benefit-or-burden.

Tea Time eBooks. *Life Lessons: How to Develop a Life You Truly Have a Passion for*. Barnes and Noble, 2013. Nook Press eBook.

Westside Toastmasters, for Public Speaking and Leadership Education, "Chapter 10: The Rule of Expectations— The Impact of Suggestion." Accessed August 23, 2013. http://westsidetoastmasters.com/resources/laws_persuasion/chap10.html.

Whitbourne, Susan K. Psychology Today, "Motivation: The Why's of Behavior." Last modified October 29, 2011. Accessed August 23, 2013. http://www.psychologytoday.com/blog/fulfillment-any-age/201110/motivation-the-why-s-behavior.

YouTube video, "Jeff Bliss, a High School student, gives a lesson to his teacher." 1:27, posted by "Bloo Dev," May 12, 2013, http://www.youtube.com/watch?v=Jo9WPkJsBLE